seventeen
How To Be Gorgeous

seventeen

How To Be Gorgeous

the ultimate **BEAUTY GUIDE** to **MAKEUP, HAIR, and MORE**

by **ELIZABETH BROUS**
beauty director of **seventeen**

A **PARACHUTE PRESS BOOK**   **HarperCollins**Publishers

Created and produced by
PARACHUTE PUBLISHING, L.L.C.
156 Fifth Avenue, Suite 302
New York, NY 10010

Published by
HarperCollins*Publishers*
1350 Avenue of the Americas
New York, NY 10019

For information write:
Editorial Manager
seventeen
850 Third Avenue
New York, NY 10022

Design by Bill Anton / Service Station
Front cover photograph by Jon Ragel
Printed in Belgium by Proost International Book Production
Separations by Jen Mar Graphics, Totowa, New Jersey

Library of Congress Cataloging-in-Publication-Data

Brous, Elizabeth.
   How to be gorgeous: the ultimate beauty guide to makeup, hair, and more:
   by Elizabeth Brous—1st ed.
     p. cm.—(Seventeen)
   ISBN 0-06-440871-X (pbk.)
   1. Beauty, Personal. 2. Cosmetics. I. Title. II. Series.

RA778.B877 2000   00-37032
646.7'2—dc21   CIP
                                          AC

10 9 8 7 6 5 4 3 2 1

First Edition

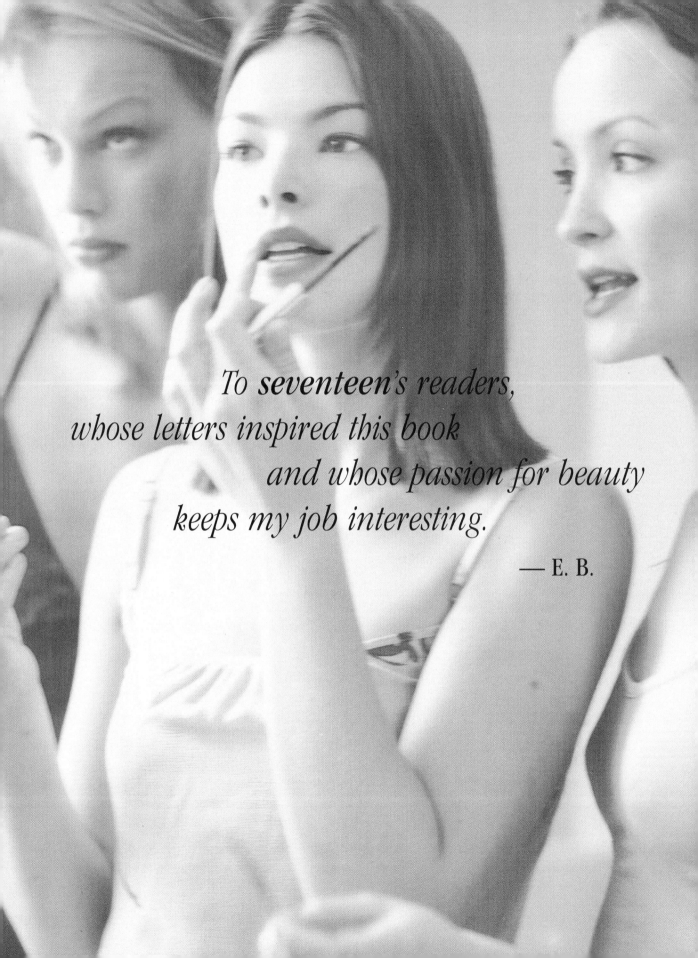

To **seventeen**'s readers,
whose letters inspired this book
and whose passion for beauty
keeps my job interesting.

— E. B.

6

Contents

chapter 3
SKIN CARE

Skin Magic 99
Figure out your skin type and how to care for it to get gorgeous, glowing skin.

Coming Clean 104
The right way to wash your face.

Saving Face 106
The best bets for beating breakouts.

Making Scents 112
The scoop on banishing body odor. Finding the fragrance that's right for you.

Bare Essentials 116
Hair removal made easy—the pros and cons of every method—and the skinny on sensitive subjects like bikini bumps, cellulite, and stretch marks.

Sun Smarts 122
The tan commandments for safeguarding your skin and how to fake a fabulous tan.

Spa Treatments 128
Have a spa party with your friends: facials, mud treatments, body polishing.

Skin Cheat Sheet 133
Quick tips for scoring clear, beautiful skin.

chapter 4
NAILS

Nail It 135
Get a great manicure in minutes.

Polish Pointers 140
Finger "tips" for a flawless paint job, from French manicures to freestyle nail painting.

A Rainbow Of Colors 144
Clues to choosing the right hues.

The Breaking Point 146
A trouble-shooting guide to scoring a perfect 10.

Nail Helpers 148
Go with the faux—how to give your natural nails an artifical boost.

Treat Your Feet 150
Pointers for a positively perfect pedicure.

Nails Cheat Sheet 153
Quick tips for nailing dashing digits.

Afterword 154
Index 155
Acknowledgments 158

Introduction

Lots of people think that beauty editors are *born* with total beauty knowledge. Well, not me! In fact, when I first started reading **seventeen**, I was completely clueless about beauty. I couldn't wait to flip open a new issue to see what my favorite models and celebs were doing with their hair and makeup. I wanted to learn the new beauty secrets and test-drive all the cool hair and makeup looks. I tied my ponytail with Saran Wrap (way before the Scrunchie was invented) and dotted on faux freckles with eyeliner (don't ask!). My makeovers may not have looked too magical back then, but I certainly had fun.

Now, after all my years as **seventeen**'s beauty director, I've discovered the most important beauty secret of all. Beauty isn't about being trendy or about looking like your favorite celeb. Beauty is about experimentation—exploring the possibilities and finding what looks best on you. And once you decide what makes you feel beautiful, it's about learning how to create that look and really play it up.

But don't get me wrong. I'm not saying you have to stick to the "right-for-you" look that you discovered last year, or last month, or even last week. As your style evolves and changes, your beauty look should morph along with it. Experimenting is what's fun.

What definitely *isn't* fun is stressing out about your frizzy or flat hair, the epic zit in the middle of your forehead, or your bushy eyebrows. If you're anything like I was, you have dozens of questions about your hair, your skin, your make-up—what to use, how to apply it, what works, and what doesn't.

That's where this book comes in. I've crammed it with all the crucial beauty tips and tricks **seventeen** has gathered over the years. I've talked to all the pros— from makeup artists to models, from celeb hairstylists to skin specialists. What's more, I've packed this book with the answers to your most-asked questions, and even tossed in tons of cool beauty tips from **seventeen** readers just like you.

You don't need to read this book from beginning to end—just pick it up and start wherever you like. Read whatever interests you that day, whether you're trying to create sexy, smoky eye makeup or just wondering how to push back your cuticles. Keep your copy wherever you stash your beauty stuff and break it open in case of an emergency. Use it as a reference guide when you're throwing a spa party for your friends or experimenting with hair color for the first time. But most of all, use it as a beginning—a starting place to explore the endless possibilities in getting gorgeous.

Elizabeth Brous

ELIZABETH BROUS
beauty director of **seventeen**

MAKEUP

chapter 1

Which Hues Are You?

Stop by our offices at **seventeen**'s headquarters, and you'll think you've gone straight to makeup heaven. The shelves are crammed with every beauty product imaginable—from sparkly glitter dust to exotically scented gloss. The best part? They're all for the trying! And that's what makeup should be about—playing with colors and having fun.

At **seventeen**, we receive thousands of "Dear Beauty Editor" letters and e-mails each month—and more than half are about finding the right makeup colors! This chapter is all about helping you find the best colors for your skin tone.

Finding the right colors for your complexion is the first step to nailing a pretty, natural makeup look. And here's more good news: You can almost always find a variation of a shade you like that will work with your skin tone.

A guide to your true colors

Take red lipstick, for example. You see a magazine picture of a beautiful model wearing a bright crimson lipcolor. It looks so cool and sophisticated against her pale skin. The prob? You're a redhead with freckles, and you've always heard that red lipstick clashes big-time with your hair color.

Not necessarily. Red can work—if you find the right red. A brown-based red with golden shimmer will most likely look great on you and help you get that dramatic look.

The easiest way to find your perfect colors is to determine which category your skin tone falls into—then practice some trial and error. The guidelines that follow are divided by the color of your skin and hair—not the origins of your ancestors.

FAIR MAIDENS

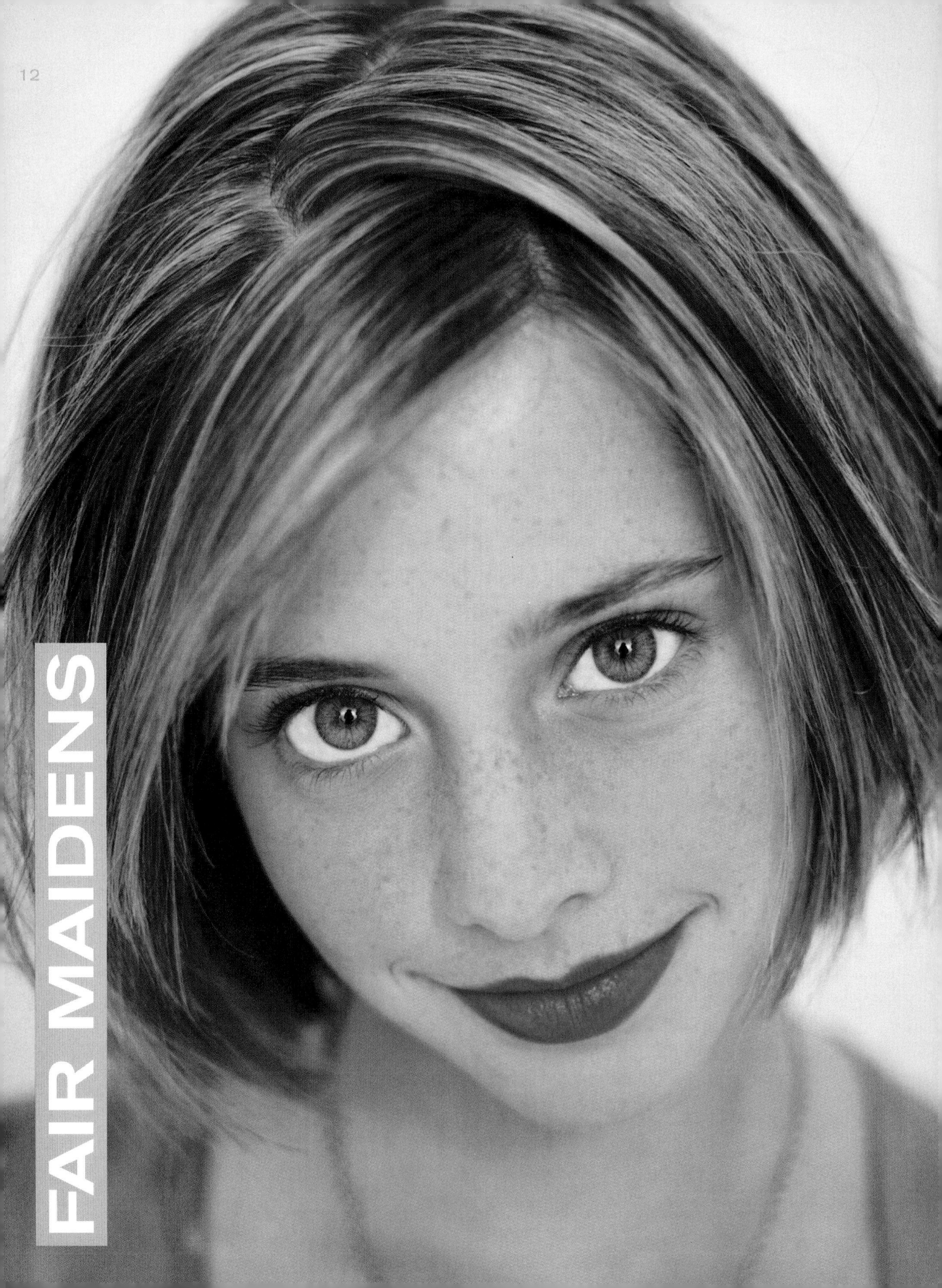

Pale-Faced Girls Look Best In Soft, Subtle Hues That Enhance Their Delicate Coloring.

Base basics:

- If your hair is blond or brown, choose foundations with an ivory or slightly yellow cast.

- Redheads should opt for neutral-toned (less yellow) foundations and concealers.

Eyes, cheeks, and lips:

- Golden-blondes and redheads usually look best in pale, warm hues like peach and coral.

- Auburn-haired girls can go for darker bronze and copper shadows, apricot or tawny blushes, and raisin or reddish-brown lipcolors.

- If your skin has a rosy cast (you blush very easily!), stay with pinks and lavenders.

Still in doubt? Neutral pinkish browns are a safe bet on all fair skins. Try soft mauve on your eyes, dusty rose tones on your cheeks, and plums, red-browns, or mauve-pinks on your lips.

Major don'ts:

- Skip really bright hues on your eyes, cheeks, and lips—they tend to look clownlike on fair skin.

- Steer clear of inky-black mascara if your lashes are pale. A softer brown or brown-black shade can give you a darkening effect without looking too harsh.

GOT FRECKLES?

Don't try to hide your freckles under loads of makeup—your skin will tend to look gray and pasty. Instead, try a sheer, tinted moisturizer that will blend in freckles a bit without covering them up altogether.

"Less is definitely more. Piling on the makeup just hides your features. Instead, find the shades that accent them."

— ROBYN, Ontario, Canada
seventeen reader

Yellow-Based Complexions Are Flattered By Earthy Tones.

GOLDEN GIRLS

Base basics:

- Go for foundation with a yellow cast—anything pink or rosy will look too obvious and will be difficult to blend.

- Try a powder with a slight yellow tint. It will look more natural than a translucent powder (a pale, almost colorless powder that tends to look too chalky or gray against golden or darker skin tones).

- If you use concealer, go one shade lighter than your skin tone for camouflaging zits, or two shades paler to conceal undereye circles.

Eyes, cheeks, and lips:

- If your golden skin is on the pale side, test-drive a muted rose or—if you're feeling dramatic—a true red lipstick.

- If your golden skin has a lot of yellow in it, stick with warmer reds, peaches, or corals.

- Rich earth tones always work on golden skin. Experiment with bronze and gold on your eyes, rosy plums on your cheeks, and pale pinks or plums with red or mauve undertones on your lips.

Major don'ts:

- Pass on bright pink, orange, or purple lip and cheek colors—they look way too unnatural.

DID U KNOW? In Ancient Egypt, skillfully applied kohl eyeliner signified that you were a member of the upper class. During ultrapious medieval times and the megaprudent Victorian era, "face paint" was considered vulgar and was worn only by actors and actresses for the stage.

OLIVE YOU

DID U KNOW? Lipstick is America's favorite cosmetic.
An estimated 75 to 80 percent of women in the United States wear it.

Olive-Skinned Girls Can Neutralize The Green With Deep, Warm Shades.

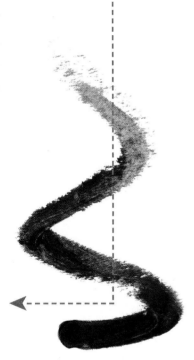

Base basics:

- Olive skin has mostly yellow undertones, so it's best to stick to yellow-tinted or neutral beige foundation.

- Pick a powder that matches your foundation—anything too light can look chalky against deeper olive skin.

- When it comes to concealer, choose one that matches your skin tone or is no more than one shade lighter. Olive-skinned girls have a tendency toward dark undereye circles. A too-light concealer can make the area look grayish instead of blending it in.

Eyes, cheeks, and lips:

- Girls with deeper skin tones can pull off darker, more intense makeup colors. Ice-cream pastels tend to look too wishy-washy.

- Shadows in deep blues and greens, as well as soft browns and grays, make dark eyes dramatic.

- Peachy-bronze or brown-based rose blushes complement olive complexions.

- Lips look great in brightly colored, sheer glosses in warm tones like copper, red-brown, and orange-red.

Major don'ts:

- Don't try to "correct" olive skin's green factor by using foundation that's pinkish or rosy. Instead, warm up your skin tone with blush (but avoid blue-based fuchsia, pink, and purple hues). Circle blush on the apples of your cheeks, then dust across your forehead, chin, and nose.

Darker Skins Get Glowing With Rich, Vibrant Colors Or Shimmery Neutrals.

RAVEN BEAUTIES

EVEN-OUT

Deeper skin tones may be more prone to unevenness and discoloration left behind by blemishes. That means they can appear lighter in some places on the face (like your cheeks and nose) and darker in others (usually around the hairline). If your complexion is two-toned, try to pick a foundation that either matches your dominant shade, or represents the average between the lighter and darker areas.

Base basics:

- If your skin tone is at the lighter, bronzer end of the spectrum, go for yellow-based foundations.

- Medium to dark complexions look best in red-based hues.

- Very deep skin tones, such as ebony, often have a bluish cast and are flattered by more neutral hues.

- To conceal blemishes, go for a deep, golden-based concealer.

- If undereye circles are a problem, try a different concealer with an orange-toned base.

- Choose a powder that's one to two shades lighter than your own hue (a darker powder could look muddy once it mixes with your skin's natural oils).

Eyes, cheeks, and lips:

- The deeper your skin tone, the more intense your makeup colors can be.

- Deep, vibrant shades (like plum, blackberry, burgundy, and aubergine) look great on lids and lips.

- Intense shadow shades like terra-cotta, purple, and chocolate-brown play up dark eyes.

- For extra drama, try shimmery neutrals (like nude pink, beige, copper, bronze, gold, or any shade of brown). Pick one or two features to play up instead of adding a high-intensity glimmer to your whole face.

Major don'ts:

- Avoid using foundations or powders that contain titanium dioxide, a common makeup ingredient that tends to look chalky on dark skin. (Check the list of ingredients on the label or box.)

- Stay away from shadows and blushes in pale pastels or silvery hues. Both can look ashy.

QUIZ:
ARE YOU WEARING THE WRONG MAKEUP?

Sure, makeup should be all about doing your own thing and experimenting with color. But there are some shade choices and application techniques that, no matter how funky your style, never work. Answer the following questions to find out if you're guilty of any of these cosmetic crimes:

1. Lucky you—you woke up with a big red zit. You try to hide it by:
a) Dotting concealer directly on top of the spot.
b) Applying concealer all around the area.

2. You decide to wear tons of black liner and smoky shadow. To complement the look, you:
a) Balance it by wearing an equally strong color on your lips.
b) Keep the focus on your eyes by applying a pale, neutral lipcolor.

3. The right shade of foundation:
a) Matches your skin tone and "disappears" when you apply it.
b) Is a shade rosier than your skin, to warm up your complexion.

4. You want your eye color to really pop, so you pick a shadow that is:
a) The same color as your eyes.
b) The complementary, or opposite, color from your eyes.

5. The fairer your skin tone...
a) The more intense your makeup colors should be.
b) The paler your makeup colors should be.

6. You want to make your thin lips look fuller, so you apply:
a) A pale, shimmery gloss.
b) A matte lipstick in a deep, intense color such as red or burgundy.

7. To streak-proof your powder blush, you:
a) First put on a bit of moisturizer to help it blend better.
b) Pat on face powder before applying it.

8. Lining your eyes inside the lower rim makes them look:
a) Bigger.
b) Smaller.

9. Everyone should wear black mascara.
a) True
b) False

SCORING:

1. (a) The best way to camouflage a zit is to apply concealer only where it's red. Ringing the spot with excess concealer will draw even more attention to it!

2. (b) According to the pros, if you're going to wear strong color, it's best to limit it to one feature at a time. Doing the smoky eye/red lip thing is likely to produce results that are more clownlike than cool.

3. (a) Any kind of camouflage makeup, whether it's foundation, concealer, or powder, should match your skin tone as closely as possible. If you want to warm up your complexion, do it with blush or bronzing powder.

4. (b) Enhancing eyes with the opposite color will make them appear brighter. For example, blue eyes look bluer next to orange-brown shadow than they do surrounded by blue shadow.

5. (b) As a general rule, pale colors are more flattering—not to mention more natural looking—on fair skin, while darker skin tones look best in deeper or brighter shades.

6. (a) Pale, shimmery colors reflect light better and give the illusion of fullness. Dark, matte shades tend to have the opposite effect.

7. (b) Powder blush tends to stick to anything "wet" (like foundation or, even worse, moisturizer). To nix streaks, dust on face powder before applying your blush.

8. (b) Not only does lining on the inside rim make your eyes look smaller, but it can also lead to eye infections.

9. (b) False. If you have fair hair and light-colored lashes, brown mascara looks more natural than inky black.

Your Makeup Routine

Does the order in which you apply your makeup really matter? Not necessarily, but sticking to these practical guidelines when you plan your makeup routine may help you avoid pitfalls such as streaking and smudging:

1 Start with a clean face. If your skin has any dry areas, apply a light layer of moisturizer.

2 Apply concealer to your undereye area and any blemishes.

3 Smooth on foundation. If some of your concealer rubs off, dot a bit more on top.

4 After applying liquid foundation, dust a translucent powder on top to set it.

5 If there's a particular area you'd like to emphasize, such as eyes or lips, make up that feature first. Then you can see how much— or how little—makeup you need on your other features.

6 When applying eye makeup, start with shadow, follow with liner, then curl your lashes. To reduce the chance of smudging, add mascara last.

7 Apply a nude liner before lipstick. Lipliner provides a goof-proof outline of the shape you want—and protects against lipstick "bleeds."

DID U KNOW? The word "makeup" was once reserved for the thick theatrical stuff actresses wore on the stage and screen. It wasn't until movie makeup artist Max Factor introduced his line of lipsticks, concealers, and powders for the public that everyday cosmetics began to be called makeup.

CONCEALER

What it's for: Camouflaging skin problems like undereye circles, blemishes, scars, veins, and any other discolorations.

Which type is right for you?

- **Liquids** that go on with a wand (or your fingertip) are easy to blend.

- **Creams** provide heavy-duty coverage.

- **Sticks** and **pencils** are perfect for covering small areas. (To avoid that cakey look, apply lightly!)

How To Apply:

To hide zits and other discolored spots:

1   Pick a hue that matches your skin tone as closely as possible. If blemishes are on the red side, a golden-based concealer shade will help neutralize the red. Pass on the true yellow, bright green, or lavender "color corrective" concealers designed to cancel out red or bluish areas. They're tough to blend and often require skillfully applied foundation on top to look natural.

2   Dot a light layer of concealer directly on top of the spot with a clean lipliner brush or your fingertip.

3   Blend the edges, then reapply if more coverage is needed.

4   Set the concealer by dusting with tinted loose powder.

 MAKEUP ARTIST SECRET: *Prime the undereye area first with a bit of moisturizer to make blending easier. If your concealer looks cakey, dab on a tiny bit of moisturizer and blend.*

What causes those dark circles under my eyes?

While undereye circles tend to be hereditary, the delicate skin in this area is also super-sensitive to external factors like pollution, allergies, sun exposure, even crying. As a result of these irritations, purplish pigment and red blood cells build up under your eyes, causing dark circles. When you stay up late, your body has less time to repair this undereye damage, so you're more likely to wake up with raccoon eyes.

For undereye circles:

1 Pick a shade that's slightly lighter than your skin.

2 Use your fingertip, the wand that comes with the product, or a flat concealer brush to apply with light, feathery strokes.

3 Pat and blend with your fingertip, working from the inner to the outer corner of each eye. (Be sure to include the area just under your lower lashes.)

FOUNDATION

▲ **What it's for:** Giving skin a more even, flawless appearance.

Which type is right for you?

- **Tinted moisturizers** are great for girls with normal to dry skin that needs minimal coverage.

- Oil-free, matte-finish **liquids** are perfect for oily skin and are easy to blend.

- **Cream-to-powder** formulas are great for all skin types and smooth on in a nanosecond with their built-in sponges.

- **Sticks** offer great spot coverage on all skin types except oily or acne-prone. Creamy sticks contain extra oils that may clog pores.

- **Dual-finish powders** are superversatile. You get different degrees of camouflage depending on how you apply them.

How To Apply:

Tinted moisturizers or liquids

1 Dot on your cheeks, nose, forehead, and chin.

2 Blend gently outward toward your hairline with your fingertips or a latex sponge (dampen the sponge for a more "sheer" effect). Use a feather-light touch—rubbing too hard removes the color.

Cream-to-powder formulas

- Apply with a dry sponge (most are packaged with one), and blend carefully around your hairline and jawline.

Sticks

- Dab sparingly on dark or red areas (cheeks, chin, the sides of your nose and mouth), then blend with a sponge.

Dual-finish powders

1. Stroke on lightly with a dry sponge for minimal coverage.

2. For more camouflage, dampen the sponge (this gives the product the coverage of a liquid).

Unless foundation has a built-in matte finish (like dual-finish powders, cream-to-powder formulas, and some liquids), set the foundation by dusting over with loose powder.

MAKEUP ARTIST SECRET: *Avoid a masklike line at your jaw by blending your makeup with a moistened latex sponge. Or apply a tiny bit of moisturizer on top of the foundation and blend the foundation over your jaw.*

I just used a self-tanning lotion, so my skin is a little darker than it usually is. Should I change my makeup to go with my bronzed look?

It's a good idea, since your everyday makeup routine may not be suited to your summer skin tone. If you wear foundation, your regular shade may be too light once your skin is bronzer. Try mixing your foundation with a few drops of liquid bronzer or bronzing gel, or switch to a sheer, tinted moisturizer that's one or two shades darker than your foundation. Since self-tanning lotions give skin a golden glow, avoid cool-toned makeup colors (blue-based purples and pinks) and opt for warm brown, peachy, or golden shades. Replace your blush with a bronzing powder, and finish with a lipcolor that flatters your summer face, like a coppery gloss.

COLD WAR

YOU'RE COUGHING. YOU'RE SNEEZING. But just because you feel sick, it doesn't mean you have to *look* sick. Here's how to deal when you're under the weather:

- To minimize a **red nose**, gently dab on a yellow-toned concealer with your fingertip. If the skin around your nostrils is flaky and peeling from blowing your nose a thousand times, massage in a rich moisturizing cream or a bit of petroleum jelly before applying any concealer.

- To warm up flu-induced **sallow skin**, dust a warm, rosy blush across your cheeks, nose, chin, and forehead. Don't try to zap the green with a pinker foundation. You're better off matching concealer and base to your skin tone.

- **Cold sores** or **fever blisters** are caused by a virus called herpes simplex type 1 (not to be confused with genital herpes, which is a sexually transmitted disease). If you get a cold sore, ask your doctor to prescribe a topical medication that may help speed up the healing process. In the meantime, keep the area clean and dry, and try to avoid covering it with makeup.

What it's for: Absorbing and controlling excess shine, setting makeup (foundation, concealer, creamy shadows) to make it last longer.

Which type is right for you?

- The pros swear by **loose powder** for creating the lightest, most natural-looking effect.

- **Pressed powder** is neater and more portable—easy to tote in your bag for touch-ups. Skip it if you are acne-prone—pressed powder contains oils to maintain its shape, so it has more potential to clog your pores than the loose variety.

- One-shade-fits-all **translucent powders** work well on lighter skin tones.

- **Tinted powders** are a better bet for medium to dark complexions. They come in a range of skin tone–matching hues.

How To Apply:

Loose powder

- Dust on loose powder with a fluffy powder brush. Tap the brush on the back of your hand first to eliminate any excess powder.

Pressed powder

- Pat on pressed powder with a velour puff.

POWDER

"To make your makeup last longer, keep your hands away from your face. Makeup will come off if you rub or pick at it!"

— KRISTEN, Washington
seventeen reader

MAKEUP ARTIST SECRET: *Choosing the wrong shade of powder—too light or too dark—can make powder more noticeable than you'd like.*

powdering their noses with plain old flour.

Medieval women did not have sleek compacts or velvety puffs, but that didn't stop them from

What it's for: Adding a rosy glow of color to pale, sallow, or washed-out cheeks.

Which type is right for you?

- **Powders** work best on normal to oily skin and are easiest to blend.
- **Creams** and **sticks** deliver a dewy, glowing finish—perfect for girls who wear minimal foundation or powder. They work best on foundation-free skin.
- **Gels** give a pretty, translucent flush. Remember, a little bit goes a long way. If you're not used to gel, be careful not to use too much—you don't want to look too rosy!

How To Apply:

For the most natural look, don't try to "create" cheekbones. Instead, apply blush to the apples of your cheeks. (To hit the right spot, smile while looking into a mirror. The part of your cheek that comes forward is the apple.)

Powder

- Before applying powder blush, prep skin by dusting translucent or tinted powder on top of your foundation. Powder blush is prone to streaking if applied to a wet or creamy surface. Dip a tapered blush brush into the blush compact (a flat powder brush picks up too much color), tap off the excess, then circle on lightly. Without redipping, use the brush to blend blush toward your ears, then downward from the apples of your cheeks toward your jaw.

Creams, sticks, or gels

- Dab creams, sticks, or gels on bare skin in small dots to avoid streaking. Blend with your fingertips. Gels tend to set quickly, so blend immediately after applying to prevent the dot pattern from staying put. If your skin is on the dry side, apply a light layer of moisturizer to help the color glide on evenly.

BLUSH

DID U KNOW? During colonial times, blush was made from crushed-up beetle shells.

 MAKEUP ARTIST SECRET: *To tone down too-bold blush, pick up some of the extra color with a clean velour powder puff, or dust face powder on top.*

What it's for: Perfecting your pout with color, shimmer, or shine.

Which type is right for you?

- **Lipsticks** come in lots of finishes (matte, creamy, shimmery, sheer, and semiglossy) and all kinds of built-in benefits (sunscreen, lip conditioners, breath fresheners, long wear). For a major color burst, go for an opaque matte or cream formula. For less color and extra moisturizing, choose a sheer or semigloss finish.

- **Slim crayons** or **liners** are perfect for shaping the outline of your mouth.

- **Lip glosses** are great for the lipstick-challenged. Because they're either totally translucent or contain only a hint of tint, you don't have to worry about "staying in the lines." The superslick formulas deliver serious shine, great lip conditioning, and funky flavors. *The downside:* Glosses don't last as long as lipstick.

LIPCOLOR

THE COLOR CODE

To make thin lips look plumper, use paler, shinier hues.

To make full lips look thinner, go for darker, more matte shades.

If you're after a natural look, choose a neutral, brown-based color that's one shade darker than the color of your lips.

If you have braces, stick to something sheer, pale, and moisturizing (a metal mouth tends to make lips dry and chapped).

How To Apply:

Lipstick

1. The easiest way to put on lipstick is straight from the tube. For more control—especially when you're using less forgiving bright or dark shades—makeup pros suggest stroking on color with a small lip brush.

2. To help matte lipstick go on smoothly (or if your lips are especially parched), moisten your kisser with a bit of lip balm first.

3. To give lipstick staying power, outline lips with a nude liner. Don't redraw the shape—your own lips will look the most natural. Use the side of the pencil to fill in your mouth, then brush on lipstick.

Lip crayon or pencil

1. If you want to wear a lip crayon solo, prep your mouth with a clear balm or gloss first.

2. Start coloring at the center of each lip and work out toward the edges. Use the side of the pencil to add more color to the center of your lips, then rub them together to blend the color.

Lip gloss

1. To help gloss linger longer, choose a gooier formula. Those that come with wands or in pots have better cling control than sticks or balms.

2. Apply gloss to your bottom lip with a wand or your fingertip, then smack your lips together—the pressure makes the slippery stuff last.

"To make your own lip gloss, mix some Vaseline with an old eye shadow or blush." — ABBY, Minnesota
seventeen reader

MAKEUP ARTIST SECRET: *If you goof, smile! (That'll stretch your lips and show where you messed up). Remove out-of-bounds color with a damp cotton swab.*

What it's for: Adding depth, definition, and color to eyes.

Which type is right for you?

- **Powders** are easy to apply and experiment with.

- **Creams** give a glossier, wetter-looking finish and tend to be more vibrant in color.

- **Sticks** tend to be long-lasting but set quickly, making them difficult to blend.

- If you wear contact lenses, opt for matte powder shadows that say "hypoallergenic" on the label. Creamy shadows contain more oil, so they're harder to remove from lenses. Tiny reflective particles in shimmery powders can get trapped in your lenses and scratch your corneas (ouch!).

How To Apply:

EYE SHADOW

- Stroke shadow on with an eye-shadow brush or sponge-tip applicator.

- Apply cream shadow with your fingertip. If shadow collects in the creases of your lids, smooth on a tiny bit of foundation or a matte powder shadow before applying the color. Like lipsticks, creamy shadow sticks have slanted tips designed to glide shadow directly onto skin.

MAKEUP ARTIST SECRET:
Before brushing on powder shadow, prep eyelids with a dusting of face powder. That way shadow won't cling to any oily areas.

Eye Openers

Eye shadow can be soft and subtle or way dramatic, depending on how you apply it. It can also be used to "reshape," giving eyes the illusion of being bigger, wider apart, or closer together.

- For the most natural look, pick one neutral shade (like vanilla, light brown, or medium brown, depending on your skin tone) and dust it lightly over your eyelids.

- For a more dramatic look, brush a medium-toned shade all over your lids. Apply a deeper shade in the crease just under your brow bones. Highlight brow bones with a pale, shimmery hue.

- Make small eyes look larger by sweeping a pale shadow over the entire lid from lashes to brow bones. (Black, brown, or gray shadow tends to make small eyes look smaller.)

- Make close-set eyes appear wider apart by applying a pale shadow to the inner half of the upper eyelid. Blend with a deeper shade toward the outer corner.

- Draw wide-set eyes closer together by shading the inner corners with darker shadow. Blend into a lighter shade at the outer corners.

When it comes to color, most makeup artists recommend intensifying your natural eye color by choosing eye makeup in a complementary shade. (Remember the color wheel from art class?)

COLOR EYE-Q

Black, charcoal gray, or mossy green look smokin' on girls with brown eyes.

Deep plums and purples light up green eyes.

Hazel eyes appear bluer in navy and greener in brown.

Blue or gray eyes smolder with coppers, browns, or a more dramatic navy.

When in doubt, go for deep, warm brown—it's flattering with any eye color!

Is your eye shadow supposed to match your eye color, your clothes, or what?

There are no hard-and-fast rules when it comes to eye shadow colors. The idea is to pick a shade that enhances your eyes— not your sweater or your prom dress. For a more natural look, go for a neutral hue (like sand, taupe, or brown) or a combination of those colors. To make your natural eye color look brighter, try a complementary shadow shade. If you're into edgy looks, don't be afraid to experiment with bold colors like blues, purples, and greens.

What it's for: Making eyes look bigger, more defined, and extra dramatic.

Which type is right for you?

- Smudgy **pencils** are great for creating a soft, smoky look.

- **Liquids** and their easier-to-use cousins, **felt-tips**, are perfect for scoring precise, dramatic looks.

- **Cake liners**, like matte eye shadows, can be used dry for a soft look or wet for a liquid-liner look.

- If you wear contact lenses, a soft, hypoallergenic pencil is your best bet.

How To Apply:

No matter what look you're going for, the key is getting the liner as close to your lashes as possible.

Pencil

1. Dot the liner on with short, quick strokes, starting at the outer corner and working inward (it helps prevent your liner from wobbling).

2. Blend with your fingertip or a rubber-tipped smudger (some pencils come with one on the other end, or you can buy one separately).

3. If you're going for a sexy, smoky look, line all the way around the eye, along both the top and bottom lashes.

EYELINER

MAKEUP ARTIST SECRET: *To keep liner as close to your lashes as possible, rest the point of the pencil or tip of the brush at the base of your lashes and act like you're coloring in the roots.*

Liquid or felt-tip liners

1 Draw only along the top lashes. Using a steady hand, aim the tip of the brush or point of the pen at the roots of your lashes.

2 For a mod-retro look, curve the line slightly up and out, to the outside corner of your eye.

3 Correct liquid or felt-tip liner blunders with a cotton swab dipped in makeup remover.

Cake liner or shadow

1 Brush on with a tiny, stiff, slant-tipped brush. For a deeper, more dramatic line, dampen the brush first and stick to the upper lashes only.

Liner safety

1 Avoid lining the inside rim of your lashes. Besides the obvious peril of poking yourself in the eye, you can clog your tear ducts and cause sties—those itchy, reddish bumps that pop up along the lash line.

2 Be sure to keep pencils clean and bacteria-free by sharpening frequently, and never share pencils with a friend.

Like shadow, eyeliner can be used to create the illusion of a different eye shape or enhance your eyes' natural shape, depending on the technique you use.

BETWEEN THE LINES

MAKE SMALL EYES LOOK BIGGER by lining along your upper lashes with a dark shade, then smudging a pale, shimmery shade beneath your lower lashes.

To MAKE CLOSE-SET EYES LOOK FARTHER APART, draw a very thin line at the inner corners of your eyes, making the line gradually thicker as it reaches the outer corners. Put this process in reverse to MAKE WIDE-SET EYES LOOK CLOSER!

MAKE DEEP-SET EYES STAND OUT by using pearly, light-colored liner along your upper lashes.

GIVE ASIAN EYES EXTRA DEFINITION by drawing a thick line with a dark matte eye shadow or cake liner.

as crushed-up plant stems and ant eggs!

DID U KNOW? Talk about all-natural formulas: The earliest eyeliners were made from such organic ingredients

What it's for: Darkening and/or enhancing lashes.

Which type is right for you?

- **Clear formulas** give already-dark lashes a glossy, defined look. They won't leave black smudges behind, and they can double as brow-tamers.

- **Lash-darkeners** deepen the color of fair-haired girls' pale lashes without thickening or lengthening.

- **Lengtheners** help shorter-lashed girls fake a longer look by depositing extra pigment at the tips of lashes.

- **Thickeners** contain volumizing ingredients that stick to the sides of wimpy lashes for a plumping effect.

- **Self-curling mascaras** are great for straight-lashed girls. Their specially designed brushes flip lashes up, while their fast-drying formulas hold the curl in place.

- **Smudgeproof formulas** help avoid raccoon eyes. They won't smear or smudge from heat or rubbing.

- **Waterproof mascaras** are the best choice for swimmers (not to mention sad-movie fans!)

- **Extra-gentle formulas** are made for contact-lens wearers and people with sensitive eyes (look for the words "ophthalmologist tested" on the package).

MASCARA

MAKEUP ARTIST SECRET: *Declump lashes by carefully combing through them with either a clean mascara wand (you can buy packages of them in beauty supply stores) or a fine-toothed lash comb.*

"Put an extra coat of mascara on the tips of your eyelashes. It gives your eyes more of an almond shape and makes them look flirtier."

— ERIN, Pennsylvania
seventeen reader

How To Apply:

1. Remove the wand from the tube without pumping it (the in-and-out motion introduces bacteria into the tube).

2. Wipe any excess goo from the end of the wand with a tissue.

3. Hold the brush horizontally at the base of your lashes and use a gentle side-to-side wiggling motion while applying mascara from the roots to the tips. (One to three thin coats work better than one glopped-on thick coat.)

4. Give any mascara a lengthening boost by dusting loose face powder on the tips of your lashes. Apply a coat of mascara on top, then repeat both steps.

One lash word

- Because volumizing mascaras tend to be thicker and wetter, it's best to let the first coat dry thoroughly before applying a second coat.

- The oils in your skin may cause regular mascara to smudge under your eyes after a few hours of wear. If your skin is on the oily side, dust lids with loose face powder before applying mascara. Coat only your top lashes, or try a smudgeproof formula on your bottom lashes.

- For a real eye-opener, curl your eyelashes (look straight into the mirror, hold an eyelash curler at the base of your lashes, and press down for 5 to 10 seconds, then carefully remove the curler). Apply a few coats of black mascara, and make sure your brows are groomed—both help open up the eye area and make eyes look larger.

*D*oes it help to open your mouth when applying mascara?

Yes, but as with many scientific phenomena, no one really knows why. It probably has something to do with the fact that it's easier to keep your head steady when you keep your jaw open and breathe through your mouth. But don't worry about striking the proper mascara-applying pose. Chances are, you do it naturally anyway.

The Brow Beat

Putting on cool eye makeup without cleaning up your brows is like wearing a killer new dress with muddy sneakers. But remember: Easy does it! The goal is to look natural but groomed, not like an overplucked chicken. Here's a fail-proof, **six-step plan for do-it-yourself tweezing:**

1. Set aside time to pluck brows right after showering, or hold a hot, wet washcloth over your brows for a few minutes. (It hurts less when your pores are still open from the steam.)

2. Brush brows upward with a brow brush or an old toothbrush. This way you can see any hairs that are really out of line.

3. Use a tweezer with an angled or pointed tip (it makes it easier to grab hairs), following the natural shape of your brows. Pluck only the stray hairs underneath your natural arch, and any really obvious strays above your brow. Be careful not to do too much grooming above your brows—it's an easy way to screw up their shape! Pull in the direction that hairs grow, and pluck only one hair at a time. Midway through tweezing, pause and step back a bit from the mirror to get a better perspective on what still needs to be plucked.

4. Don't try to change the shape of your brows dramatically or create an arch that isn't there. The shape you were born with is the most flattering one for your face. If you want to enhance your own natural arch, the highest point should be about three-quarters of the way toward the end of the brow or even with the outer edge of your iris (the colored part of your eye). Brows should taper slightly from the arches to the ends. The ends should extend beyond the outer corners of your eyes.

5. If your brows are sparse, fill in gaps with a brow powder, pencil, or matte eye shadow. To give naturally dark brows a lighter appearance, try smearing a tiny bit of foundation onto a toothbrush and brushing across brows in an upward motion.

6. When finished, repeat the brushing step (Step 2) to give tweezed and filled-in brows a groomed look.

EYEBROWS

"Tame wild eyebrows with clear mascara. No one will ever know, and they stay right where you put them!"

— MELISSA, Pennsylvania
seventeen reader

Dear seventeen.

I've got really full eyebrows. They need some shaping, but I'm scared to tweeze them because I still want them to look natural. Any tips?

Even the natural look requires some grooming. Heavier brows can grow too long, stick up, or hang down and make eyes appear droopy. Start by plucking only the obvious stray hairs underneath brows. Next, brush brows straight up with a brow brush or an old toothbrush. If the hairs are superlong and look uneven after brushing, use small, straight scissors to trim a tiny bit off the top. Cut in the direction toward your nose. Finish by brushing brows up and out toward the ends. To tame unruly hairs, use a brow gel, a bit of clear mascara, or even a dab of petroleum jelly.

WHEN TO GO TO A PRO

If you've majorly goofed and your brows have either disappeared or have more holes than Swiss cheese, a brow professional can help. Schedule a consultation at a beauty salon, but don't count on getting an instant fix: In all likelihood, a makeup artist will suggest you let brows grow in a bit before returning for a shaping, either by tweezing or waxing.

What it's for: Adding a glam gleam to anyplace you want: cheekbones, brow bones, lips—whatever!

Which type is right for you?

- **Loose shimmer powders** are superversatile. They can be brushed on alone or mixed with anything from body lotion to hair gel. But they can be very messy to use and to tote in your bag. **Pressed shimmer powders**, while not as sparkly, are a lot neater.

- **Liquid shimmers** are like pearlescent foundations. Their gleam tends to be on the subtle side, so they're great for giving an allover sheer glow.

- **Creams** have high-beam shine, so they can be a little trickier to apply. They're great for eyelids, mixing with lip gloss, and smoothing on your shoulders or throat when you're wearing a skin-baring dress.

SHIMMER

- **Sticks** are easier to control than creams and powders. They're perfect for stroking on cheekbones and body parts, but may be too heavy if your skin is oily or acne-prone.

- **Pencils** are for lining eyes. They come in both subtle frosts and in-your-face glitter versions.

How To Apply:

- Avoid your T-zone (forehead, nose, and chin) if your skin is on the oily side. Too much sparkle will just look greasy.

- Choose a shimmery shade that goes with your skin tone. In general, pearly pink shimmers look best on fair skin, silvery shades are perfect for medium complexions, and gold or copper gives dark complexions a warm glow.

- Prep eyelids with a dusting of face powder first, so the shimmer cream has something to cling to.

- Use glitter liner only outside your lash line, and skip it altogether if you wear contact lenses.

- For lustrous lips, add a dab of pearly gloss to the center of your lower lip, either on its own or on top of your regular lipstick.

- It's best to apply sparingly (you can always add more!). If you end up looking like Tinkerbell anyway, cut your losses, wash your face, and start again.

"If eyeliner looks too harsh, soften it up by applying a shimmery shadow on top of it, then sweeping the same shimmery shadow over your lid so it matches your eyeliner."

— JENNIFER, California
seventeen reader

MAKEUP ARTIST SECRET: *Don't go overboard. To get the glow—without the glare—start by adding shimmer to just one feature, like eyes or lips.*

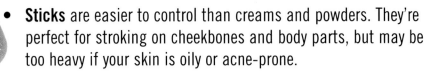

Tomorrow I'm getting my yearbook photo taken at school. The flash always makes my face look so white. Any suggestions?

Getting your picture taken is one time when you can be a little more heavy-handed with the makeup. If you normally skip the foundation and just wear concealer, try using both to create a totally flawless look. To counteract the whitening effect of the flash, try dusting a sheer layer of bronzing powder all over your face (choose as pale a shade of bronze as possible to avoid the fake suntan look). Apply face powder liberally. Anything shiny (like your T-zone) catches the light and stands out more. The same goes for gooey lip glosses and too-sparkly shadows. It's best to stick to creamy or matte finishes when you're going in front of the camera. Oh, yeah—don't forget to smile!

Do you need help scoring 20/20 vision? No big deal. A pair of funky glasses can be a cool accessory (and they can help you to actually see the blackboard from the back of bio class, which can be crucial if you plan to pass). When you're choosing your frames, the most important factor to consider is the shape of your face.

Face shape: **Oval**
What it looks like: The top half balances the bottom half.
Go for: Any shape frames, as long as they're as wide or wider than the widest part of your face.

Face shape: **Round**
What it looks like: Full cheeks, rounded forehead and chin.
Go for: Square or rectangular frames that are wider than they are deep. They'll help slim your face and add length.

Face shape: **Heart**
What it looks like: An upside-down triangle: a wide forehead and a narrow, pointed chin.
Go for: Light-colored, thin, or rimless frames that are wider at the bottom than they are on top. They'll help balance a wide forehead.

Face shape: **Oblong**
What it looks like: Long and narrow.
Go for: Round frames that are deep from top to bottom instead of elongated. To make a long nose look shorter, look for a style with a low bridge.

Face shape: **Square**
What it looks like: A wide forehead and jaw.
Go for: Rounded or curved frames that are more horizontal than vertical and are wider than the widest part of your face. They'll soften your angular chin and give your face a rounder look.

Face shape: **Diamond**
What it looks like: A small forehead, wide temple area, and small pointed chin.
Go for: Frames that are heavier on top (straight on top and curved on the bottom). They'll give you the illusion of a wider forehead that better balances your cheekbones.

MAKEUP ARTIST SECRET: *If you wear glasses, make sure your brows have a definite arch, so they don't disappear behind your frames. You might also want to intensify your eye makeup a bit: Use a pale, shimmery shadow, curl your lashes, and apply lots of mascara. If you opt for contacts, make sure any eye makeup you use is hypoallergenic and safe for lens wearers.*

A Checklist

Did you know that you were born with the best beauty tool possible? Your fingertips! But sometimes, finger painting can only take you so far. For perfecting certain application techniques (and cutting down on the mess factor), there are a few essential tools no makeup bag should be without.

Must-haves

- **Powder brush:** The larger and fluffier, the better to deliver the sheerest application of powder. It can also be used for dusting on bronzing powder.

- **Blush brush:** Smaller than a powder brush, it should be soft, with tapered edges to pick up and blend cheek color.

- **Tweezers:** They should be stainless steel with a slanted or pointed tip to make it easier to grab one hair at a time.

- **Makeup sponges:** Pick up a bag of latex makeup sponges at any drugstore or beauty supply store. Wedge-shaped ones are great for blending makeup in hard-to-reach areas.

- **Powder puff**: Get a large velour puff for patting on pressed powder or blending away excess blush.

- **Eyebrow brush/lash comb:** This combo comb can't be beat for grooming brows and de-clumping mascara.

- **Pencil sharpener:** Keeps your eyeliner and lipliner points perfect (not to mention more hygienic—each time you sharpen, you reveal a fresh, clean, bacteria-free tip underneath). Make sure your sharpener has both large and small holes to accommodate any size pencil.

Extras, extras

Add these tools to your kit if you're into the special effects they deliver:

- **Eyeliner brush:** Anyone who uses eye shadow to line her eyes needs one. It should be firm enough to draw on a fine line when dampened, with a slanted edge for extra precision.

- **Lip brush:** If you prefer dark or bright lipstick colors to transparent glosses, use this tiny, pointed brush for creating the perfect shape. *Bonus:* It's also great for dotting concealer directly on top of spots. Look for one that swivels up and retracts so you can tuck it in your bag.

TOOL TIME

TO BUY OR NOT TO BUY?

Sure, most blushes and shadows are packaged with their own tools. The problem is, you usually get what you pay for. So while a bargain-priced shadow may fit the bill when you're craving a trendy new shade, the skimpy sponge-tip applicator it comes with may be too tiny to maneuver effectively. Or the brush that you got in your new powder blush compact is made of a material that feels like doll's hair—it's too slippery to distribute any color on your cheeks. Sometimes it's a good idea to invest in better-quality—or simply full-size—tools. Spring for brushes with natural bristles, or at least a combination of natural and synthetic. Be on the lookout for bristles that feel smooth and don't shed easily. Freebie tools that do tend to get the job done: rubber-tipped smudgers on the end of your eyeliner, foam sponges that come with compact foundations, velour puffs packed inside pressed powder compacts.

- **Eye shadow brush:** Want to play Picasso with your shadow? Use this small, flat brush when you want to place powder shadow in small areas like the inner corners of your eye.

- **Rubber-tip smudger**: If your eyeliner doesn't come with one, invest in this inexpensive, slant-tipped tool for smoothing out harsh pencil lines.

- **Eyelash curler:** This nifty device gives straight lashes extra bend for an eye-opening look. Keep it clean—and protect lashes from fallout—by using your curler before applying mascara.

"To get super-curled lashes, try heating your eyelash curler with a blow-dryer before using it."

— AMANDA, New Jersey
seventeen reader

WORD OF ADVICE

Don't go for the all-inclusive, multiple-tool set. While it may seem like a good value, it's only cost-effective if you end up using all the brushes and applicators that come in the kit (and chances are, you won't!). Instead, buy tools separately, and buy only what you think you'll use. You can always add on to your tool lineup if you need to.

YOU'D NEVER REUSE THE SAME BATTER-SPECKLED SPATULA OR MEASURING SPOON EVERY TIME YOU BAKED A CAKE, RIGHT?

The same basic principle should apply to your makeup tools. You don't have to give applicators a scrub-down every time you use them, but if you can't remember the last time you cleaned them, it's probably time. Here's how:

- **Wash makeup brushes** at least once a month by lathering up bristles with a bit of mild soap or baby shampoo. Rinse well, then blot gently with a towel. (You can also use a blow dryer to speed up the drying process.) Allow brushes to dry flat, with their bristles hanging off the edge of a table or shelf. Leaving them upright can cause moisture to leak into the handles, which leads to warping.

- **Wash makeup sponges** frequently in warm, soapy water. Leave them out where they can air-dry completely before storing them in an enclosed space, like a drawer or compact.

- **Sharpen eye and lip pencils** after every few uses.

- **Clean metal tools** (like tweezers and nail scissors) with alcohol once a month.

Light It Right

We've all been there. You try to put on blush or foundation in a dim room. Then you walk outside, and in daylight, your cheeks look clownlike and your makeup abruptly stops at your jawline. We can't emphasize enough how important good lighting is when it comes to nailing perfect makeup.

The best light for applying any kind of makeup is natural daylight. During the day, a bathroom with a window or a makeup mirror placed on a table next to a window is the locale of choice. When this isn't possible, apply makeup in the brightest light possible (such as a bare bulb), then check your results in dimmer lighting to see how your makeup will look inside the gym at a dance or in a friend's basement at a party. *Another option:* Check out the hardware store for special lightbulbs designed to mimic daylight as closely as possible, and replace the bulb in your bathroom with one.

"If you want your lipcolor to stay on longer, rub an ice cube over your lips after you apply it."

— SARAH, Maryland
seventeen reader

Dear Seventeen:

I want to start wearing makeup, but I'm not allowed to wear much. How can I create a really natural-looking face?

Stick to the bare essentials: Unless your skin needs a lot of evening out, pass on the foundation and use a sheer, tinted moisturizer all over your face. If you have undereye circles or blemishes, dot on a bit of concealer and blend well. Find a blush that matches the flush you get after exercising, and circle it on the apples of your cheeks with a blush brush. Enhance your eyes by sweeping on a light brown shadow and brushing on a coat of brown mascara (it looks less obvious than black). Finish off your face with a neutral lip gloss that's close to your natural lip color.

MAKEUP ARTIST SECRET: *Want a brighter smile? Skip any lipcolor with blue-red or cool pink undertones. Both tend to make teeth look yellower. Go for a warmer peach or brown-based berry.*

Makeup Removal

What goes on must come off…unless you want to wind up with clogged pores and irritated eyes! Resist the temptation to sleep in your makeup, no matter how late it is and how tired you are. For one thing, healthy skin depends on downtime. Skin cells restore themselves while you're sleeping. Leaving them coated with a faceful of pore-gunking makeup hinders their progress and can cause breakouts. Also, sleeping in eye makeup can lead to gnarly infections and sties. Here's how to start the night with a clean slate:

Face makeup: Sudsing up with plain old soap and water will remove most foundations, concealers, and powder. If your skin is on the sensitive side or feels dry and tight after you use soap, go for a nonsoap liquid cleanser—it helps skin retain its natural moisture balance.

Eye makeup: To take off shadow, eyeliner, and mascara that isn't water-soluble (translation: It doesn't wash off easily with mild soap and water), use an eye makeup remover. Place a cotton ball soaked with remover on your eyelid for a few seconds to help loosen the makeup. Swipe gently across your lids and lashes, then rinse well with cool water.

CLEAN UP YOUR ACT

MAKING MAKEUP LAST

- Heat and humidity from your shower can cause cosmetic meltdown in creamy products like lipsticks, cream blushes, and eye shadows. Move your moist makeup out of the bathroom and into a cool, dry place like a drawer, vanity table, or cosmetics organizer on your dresser.

- Airtight is right when it comes to products that contain alcohol (nail polishes, removers, perfumes, and so on). Since most perfumes are at least 20 percent alcohol, keeping stoppers tightly sealed means your fragrances will last longer.

- Lotions and gels with pumps keep their contents airtight and bacteria-free. That's because you don't have to keep sticking your hands in the jar!

"Try using petroleum jelly as an eye makeup remover. It gets every last bit off, moisturizes the area well, and costs next to nothing."

— SARAH, Maryland
seventeen reader

Out With The Old

Unlike milk or yogurt, most beauty products don't come with an expiration date. But that doesn't mean they'll last forever. If you're a beauty junkie, your drawers, closets, and medicine chest are probably overflowing with old lipsticks, half-used nail polishes, and way-expired self-tanning lotions.

As a general rule, **most makeup should be tossed within one year after it's been opened** to prevent bacteria from growing and spreading to your face and eyes. Here are a few exceptions:

- **Mascara:** Once opened, mascara should never be kept longer than three months. (Nasty bacteria—from your eyes and from the air pumped inside the tube each time you remove the wand—can't wait to fester inside your lash enhancer).

- **Eyeliner, eye shadow:** Trash four to six months after using it.

- **Foundation:** If you've got any left over after a year, it's time to replace it. But anything water-based is a real germ magnet, and should be tossed after six months.

- **Lip gloss:** Like mascaras, glosses with wand applicators that you apply to your mouth and stick back in the tube should be replaced after three or four months.

- **Preservative-free makeup:** Many health-food–store brands cut preservatives out of their makeup and skin-care formulas. These products have a shorter shelf life and should be tossed as soon as they show signs of breaking down.

CHUCK ANY MAKEUP NOW IF...

It's turned cakey or chalky (eye shadows, face powders, powder blushes).

It smells funny (mascaras, eye pencils, lipsticks, glosses).

It separates or thickens (liquid foundations, concealers, glosses).

It's changed color (cream blushes, foundations, concealers).

It's dried up or broken into pieces (mascaras, powder blushes, face powders, eye shadows).

You haven't used it in six months—chances are, you never will! Throw it out and make room for new stuff.

Should I keep my make-up (eyeliners, nail polish) in the refrigerator?

Keeping makeup in the fridge isn't likely to keep it fresh any longer. Unless it's the preservative-free kind from the health-food store, makeup is designed with a certain shelf life. Placing your products in the deep freeze can't change that. Do store makeup and nail polish away from humidity, in a drawer or makeup organizer box.

Okay, so you don't always have a millennium to spend lining your eyes and blending your blush—sometimes it's a matter of minutes (or even seconds, if you're late for the bus!). Here's a sample schedule for three degrees of makeup maintenance:

The Bare Essentials

You have: **Five minutes, tops**

You're going: To school, to a friend's house, to the park, to a family reunion

The routine:

- Conceal any undereye circles or blemishes.

- If your skin still looks blotchy or uneven, use a sheer, tinted moisturizer. *Bonus:* Most have a built-in SPF (sun protection factor) of 15, a must-have if you'll be outdoors.

- If you have pale lashes, apply a coat of brown or black-brown mascara.

- Finish with a lip balm or gloss.

A Little More...

You have: **Ten minutes**

You're going: To hang out at the mall, to your job in a cool boutique, on a movie date

The routine:

- As above, conceal anything that needs camouflaging.

- Dab on foundation, blending with a makeup sponge.

- Dust translucent or tinted powder on top.

- Stroke some rosy blush on the apples of your cheeks.

- Apply one shade of neutral, medium-toned shadow (taupe or brown) to your eyelids.

- Add a few thin coats of mascara.

- Brush your eyebrows up and outward with a brow brush or an old toothbrush.

- Pick a lipcolor that's one shade darker than your natural lip color. Apply with a lip brush, then add a slick of clear gloss on top.

All-Out-Glam

You have: **Fifteen to twenty minutes**

You're going: To a party, to someplace romantic with your boyfriend, to a formal dance

The routine:

- Follow the concealer, foundation, and blush steps above.

- Apply a medium-toned shadow to your eyelids, a darker shadow in the crease, and a pale shadow to your brow bones.

- Line your eyes with a dark pencil or liquid liner (or use a matte powder shadow with a dampened liner brush).

- Curl your upper lashes, then apply a few coats of black mascara.

- After plucking any stray hairs from your brows, brush brows in place and fill in any sparse areas with brow pencil or powder.

- Line and fill in lips with a nude lip pencil. Apply lipstick on top with a lip brush. Then add a coat of pearly, shimmery gloss.

- Highlight your cheekbones, brow bones, collarbones, and shoulders (if you're wearing something bare) with a shimmery powder or cream.

Help—I'm bored! I always wear all my makeup the exact same way. What quick things can I do to look different?

There are a few ways to shake up your makeup without buying a truckload of new cosmetics. For one thing, you can test-drive a new application technique. If you always wear soft brown eye shadow, try dampening a small eyeliner brush with water and painting on the same shadow as a deeper, sexier eyeliner. Another way to get a different look: Emphasize a different feature than you normally do. If you're usually big on lipcolor, try a pale neutral lipstick and play up your eyes with smoky shadow. Or tone down your heavily lined eyes and sport a deep berry lipstick. Finally, try throwing just one trendy new hue into the mix (like lavender mascara.) It'll give you a boost to beat the boredom.

Leaders Of The Pack

You may be tempted, but there usually isn't room to tote your entire cosmetics collection everywhere you go! Here's a sample packing list to help you streamline your beauty essentials for your backpack or purse:

MAKEUP ESSENTIALS

1. Pressed powder or blotting papers (for zapping midday shine).

2. Concealer (for retouching or hiding any unexpected face-invaders).

3. Lip gloss or balm (Reapply often to maintain your mouth's shine factor and moisturize chapped lips.)

4. All-in-one lip, eye, and cheek color (usually in neutral-hued cream or stick).

5. Double-ended mascara/eyeliner (saves space without sacrificing all-day perfect eye makeup).

6. Makeup wipes (Individual towlettes soaked in remover can take off migrating mascara or liner faster and more neatly than soap and water.)

7. A brown eyeliner pencil (It can double as a lipliner or a brow pencil.)

8. A few disposable latex sponges (for blending makeup that's gotten streaky or separated).

9. Purse-sized brush and minihairspray (Even if it's not your styling product of choice, flipping your head over and spritzing a bit on your roots adds instant volume to hair that falls flat after gym.)

10. Toothbrush, toothpaste, dental floss, and mouthwash (kills cafeteria-induced bad breath).

Makeup Cheat Sheet

Ready for a quick recap?
Here are the crucial points to remember when
it comes to nailing your makeup look:

- Camouflage products such as foundation, powder, and concealer should match your skin tone as closely as possible. If you want to warm up your complexion, do it with blush or bronzer instead.

- If you want to wear color that's intense, deep, or super-shimmery, pick one feature to play up. Accentuating eyes, lips, and cheeks can produce clownlike results.

- Apply eyeliner as close to your lashes as possible. For best results, pretend you're actually "coloring in" the roots.

- Give brows a groomed, but still natural look by tweezing only the stray hairs underneath. Overplucking looks totally artificial.

- Make your makeup last longer by dusting loose powder under eye shadow and over foundation, and lining lips with nude lipliner before brushing on lipcolor.

- Always apply makeup in good lighting. Daylight or a brightly lit makeup mirror are best.

HAIR

chapter 2

Which Haircut Is Right For You?

Talk about a whole new you! Nothing gives your look a bigger boost than a cool new hairstyle. Searching through magazines for the right style—by yourself or with your friends—is half the fun.

Should you go long and layered or short and blunt? Should you change your color to a coppery red or a jet black? Maybe you should wear your hair up in a romantic twist or blow your curls out so they're stick-straight. When it comes to doing a new 'do, the possibilities are endless.

But before you waltz into the salon with a picture of your favorite celebrity's latest haircut, there are a few things you need to keep in mind.

Number one: Her style is the result of hours of attention from a team of pros before the photo was ever snapped. Number two: It's not going to look the same on you unless you have the exact same face shape and hair type.

Whenever **seventeen** calls professional stylists for haircut advice, they always tell us that the first things they consider are face shape and hair type. So, to determine if your dream 'do is doable for you, you first need to see which category you fall into.

Face Shape

Pull your hair back in a headband and look into the mirror. Now decide which shape your face most resembles.

Oval: Not too wide or too narrow, balanced at the forehead and chin

Square: Broad, high forehead and a wide jaw

Round: On the full side and widest at the cheekbones

Heart: Wide at the forehead and cheekbones with a narrow, pointy chin

Long and narrow: High forehead and a long chin

Style Counsel

Oval: Oval-shaped faces can pull off just about any haircut, but check to make sure it suits your hair type.

Square: If your face is square, hair should be layered softly around your face and hang below your jaw. Chin-length bobs focus attention on a wide jaw. You can hide a broad forehead with bangs, but they should be long and softly layered instead of a short, straight-across fringe.

Round and Heart-shaped: Elongate the look of round and heart-shaped faces with longer (below the shoulders) hair that has some volume or lift at the roots. Softly angled layers around the face will minimize fullness more than blunt bangs.

Long and Narrow: To shorten a long, narrow face, try a cut that's below your chin but above your shoulders. Hair that stops above your chin makes your face look even longer. Locks that are too long drag the eye down and emphasize a narrow face. Your cut should have layers or texture built in to create more volume and movement on the sides.

THE RIGHT CUT

Hair Types

Hair types are based on two factors:
thickness (fine, medium, or coarse) and **texture** (straight, wavy, or curly).
As a general rule:

- Blond hair tends to be the finest.

- Brown hair tends to be medium to thick.

- Red hair is often the thickest and coarsest.

- Dark brown or black hair varies, depending on your ancestry:

  African-American locks tend to be fine and very curly, so they appear to be thicker and coarser.

  Asian hair tends to be straight, but each individual strand is thick, so hair has more volume than, say, superstraight blond locks.

Keep in mind that when you chemically process your hair—by coloring, perming, or relaxing it—your hair type changes, at least temporarily.

To get the scoop on your type and how to care for it, find the combo that most closely describes your tresses.

How it acts: Limp and lifeless; tends to fall flat or look "plastered down" to your head when it's dirty; if it's straight, doesn't hold curl well.

Cleansing and conditioning:

- Lather up daily with a **protein-enriched, body-building shampoo**—it coats each strand to add fullness and volume.

- Contrary to popular belief, fine hair is prone to tangle trouble, so don't skip the conditioner. Choose either a **body-building conditioner** (it contains ingredients that cling to the hair shaft to temporarily "swell" its circumference) or a **lightweight detangler**. Apply it only from the middle of the hair shaft down to the ends.

Your best haircuts: Fine hair looks fuller when it's cut shoulder length or shorter, with either blunt ends or slightly layered ends for movement.

Cool tools: A blow-dryer, a medium-size round brush, Velcro rollers, a fine-toothed comb.

Must-have products: A volumizing spray or mousse.

Styling Smarts:

- Lock in more body by applying a **volumizing spray** or **mousse** to damp hair. Comb through evenly, from roots to ends.

- For a quick volume boost, bend over, letting your hair hang forward, and blow-dry. While blow-drying, massage the roots with your fingers. Then brush your hair downward with a **medium round brush**, following the brush with heat from the dryer. Concentrate on the roots. When hair is dry, flip your head back up.

- If you have a lot of time, give hair lift with a **jumbo curling iron** or **large rollers**. To use the iron, hold a section of hair away from your head and clamp the curling iron around it at the base of your scalp. Hold for 30 seconds. Then wrap the rest of the section around the iron (not too tightly) and tuck the ends inside the clamp. Hold for another 30 seconds, then unroll.

- When working with rollers, separate almost-dry hair into one-inch sections, then wind each section around a Velcro roller (choose medium-size rollers for shoulder-length hair, large rollers for longer hair). Start with the hair at the crown (or top) of your head. Wrap up the sides and the back. When hair is all rolled, spritz lightly with volumizing spray, then direct heat from the blow-dryer at each roller. Let hair cool for a couple of minutes before removing the rollers. Gently brush locks into place.

FINE HAIR

- For extra lift on top, **tease** small sections of hair. Hold a section straight up and using a fine-toothed comb, comb down, toward the roots, with short, quick strokes. Repeat three times. Smooth the top layer of hair over the teased portions. For more permanent body-building, consider a body wave, root-lifting perm, or a hair color change (hair dye swells the hair shaft and gives fine hair more oomph).

PRO TIP: *An easy way to get a temporary lift at the roots: Change your part from one side to the other.*

How it acts: Whether it's straight or wavy, medium-thick hair tends to hold a style longer than fine hair. Its condition can be dry, normal, or oily, due in part to how you take care of it.

Cleansing and conditioning:

Shampoo:

- If hair is healthy, suds up with a **daily formula** that won't strip away natural oils.
- If hair is on the oily side, go for a **concentrated, deep-cleansing shampoo**.
- If hair is on the dry side, use a **moisturizing shampoo**.

Do you use lots of styling products? Once a week, replace your regular shampoo with a **clarifying formula** that will remove dulling buildup.

Conditioner:

- If your hair feels limp, go for a **body-building conditioner or detangler**.
- If your hair feels dry, use a **protein-rich, moisturizing conditioner**.

Your best haircuts: With medium-thick hair, just about any length works. If hair is very curly, long layers are more flattering.

Cool tools: A blow-dryer, a round brush or paddle brush, a straightening iron, Velcro rollers, metal clips for sectioning.

Must-have products: Silicone-based shine serum, straightening balm, volumizing spray or mousse, leave-in conditioner, gel.

MEDIUM HAIR

Styling Smarts:

- If you want your hair sleek, work a few drops of **silicone shine serum** into damp hair. Blow-dry while brushing sections with a **paddle brush** or **medium-size round brush**.

- If hair is curly, try mixing a **straightening balm** with your shine serum. Separate hair into sections with clips. Put the dryer on a higher heat setting, and pull sections with a **large round brush** while you blow-dry. For extra sleekness, run a **straightening iron** over already dried sections.

- To add more lift at the roots, apply **body-building spray** or **mousse** and repeat the steps for blow-drying and roller-setting fine hair.

- Give layered hair added texture by working a **leave-in conditioner** or **gel** into damp hair and blow-drying while styling with your fingers. Use a round brush to finesse face-framing areas.

Should I shampoo my hair every day no matter what? How do I know if it's dirty or not?

Your hair will tell you when it's time to suds up by looking dull, flat, and possibly, oily. If your locks are fine and/or oily, chances are you'll need to shampoo every day to keep them looking clean and add more body. If your hair is on the dry and/or coarse side, it will probably look and feel better if you lather up every other day, or even every three days (on days when you're not shampooing, simply wet hair and apply conditioner when you're in the shower). Of course, it goes without saying that if you exercise, hit the beach, or do anything else that makes you perspire, it's best to shampoo as soon as possible afterward.

DID U KNOW? The average number of hairs on the human scalp is 120,000. Blondes tend to have the most hairs, but each is small in diameter, so hair looks fine. Redheads tend to have the fewest hairs, but each strand is thicker, so their hair looks full.

How it acts: Coarse hair has plenty of body, but its texture tends to make it shine-challenged. When it's curly (as it often is), its corkscrew shape makes it delicate and prone to breakage (and even more dull, because it doesn't reflect light as well as straight hair). In addition, when hair is dry, it tends to soak up moisture from humid air like a sponge, swelling individual strands and creating a fuzzy, frizzy effect all over.

Cleansing and conditioning:

- Wash every other day (or even less often if your hair is very dry) with a gentle, **creamy shampoo with built-in conditioner** to decrease excess poufiness and add moisture.

- When you shampoo, don't pile your hair up on top of your head—it contributes to major snarls. Instead, massage your scalp gently with your fingertips.

- Conditioning is ultraimportant for restoring moisture to coarse hair. Choose a **protein-packed formula**, and gently comb it through hair with a wide-toothed comb. After rinsing, blot dry with a towel (nix the rubbing, to prevent frizz). Comb through again, holding sections with your hands so the comb doesn't yank too much and cause breakage. Once a week, apply a **deep conditioner**.

Your best haircuts: Styles that are shoulder length or longer tend to work better (shorter looks can pouf out and go triangular). Hair should be cut in long, graduated layers to remove some of the bulk from the ends. Stay away from too-short layers. They can give coarse or curly hair a bubblelike look. If hair is curly, make sure your stylist allows for shrinkage when he or she is cutting (dried hair springs up way shorter than wet hair, which can be a major factor in cutting bangs).

Cool tools: A wide-toothed comb, a blow-dryer. For straight hair: a paddle brush. For curly hair: a diffuser attachment for your dryer, a curling iron.

Must-have products: A balm or leave-in conditioner, a mousse or gel/mousse, a silicone shine serum, a soft-hold gel.

Styling Smarts:

- If your hair is **coarse** and **straight**, work in a **leave-in conditioner** and blow-dry in sections, pulling down with a **paddle brush**.

- If hair is **coarse** and **curly**, choose your styling products based on your degree of curliness or frizz. If you're not sure which product is right for you, test-drive a few or try a combo to see what works best. (FYI: Stick to alcohol-free formulas if your hair is dry, since alcohol can dry out hair even more.)

  - Use a **balm** or **leave-in conditioner** for smoothing humidity-induced frizz out of wavy hair.
  - Try a **mousse** or **combo gel/mousse** for controlling and defining curls without zapping all your natural volume.
  - Go for a **silicone-based shine serum** for de-frizzing and adding shine to dull hair.
  - Use a **soft-hold gel** for superdefined curls and major hold.

- While your hair is still damp, arrange curls the way you want them to look. Refine ringlets at the hairline by wrapping them around your fingers. Whenever possible, allow hair to air-dry, and don't mess with it while it's drying. The less you do to your curls (including brushing them, which ups the frizz factor), the better they'll look.

- If you must blow-dry, attach a **diffuser** to your dryer. A diffuser reduces the strength of the airflow, which can pull out the curl. Keep your head upright while you style—flipping your hair over or from side to side will give it extra volume.

"Add definition to curls by towel-drying freshly-shampooed hair, then kind of messing up your locks like you're scrubbing your scalp. Immediately after, gather your hair into a messy updo without brushing it. Once hair is almost dry, take it down and allow to air-dry loose."

— TAYLOR, Illinois
seventeen reader

Dear seventeen:

The directions on my bottle of conditioner say to leave it in for 3 minutes. Will it work better if I leave it in for 15 minutes?

It won't hurt to leave conditioner on your hair for longer than the directions say, but it probably won't help, either. Instant conditioners are formulated to be just that—hair absorbs as much as it's going to absorb within a few minutes. Deep conditioners are another story. They contain a different mix of proteins and humectants (this helps to hold in moisture) that's meant to be left on your hair for longer—usually ten to fifteen minutes.

DID U KNOW? A healthy hair is stronger than copper wire of the same thickness. An average head of hair can support up to twenty-three tons of weight. (Do not try this trick at home!)

I'm Sooooo Bored With My Hair!

Maybe the feeling was brought on by a bad hair day. Maybe you came across an old kindergarten photo and realized, with horror, that you haven't really changed your hair since your *Sesame Street* days. No matter what triggered it, you know that if you don't get a completely new hairstyle within the hour, you'll go totally postal. You race to the salon, throw yourself at the mercy of your stylist…and then, suddenly, that cute pixie cut seems kind of, well, drastic.

Chill out—you don't have to cut off all your options (or all of your hair) to get a really different look. Here are seven not-so-major changes to try before submitting to the scissors:

1 **Change your texture.** Temporary texture changes are an easy, commitment-free way to satisfy the need for a new look. If your hair is straight, try making spiral curls with a curling iron. If you have curls, use some straightening balm and a big round brush and blow-dry them straight.

2 **Get an intermediate cut.** Yes, scissors are involved, but it isn't as dramatic as a total chop—and it's a lot easier to cope with than seeing ten inches of hair fall to the floor. An intermediate cut—like a layered bob—lets you test-drive shorter hair, but still leaves you with some length to play with. If you're still stuck on a shorter style after living with the medium length for a few weeks, go for it.

3 **Get bangs.** Cutting bangs isn't as scary as chopping it all off. Bangs can be anywhere from schoolgirl-short to long, layered, and sideswept. Shorter, thicker bangs work best on oval-shaped faces. Softer, longer bangs flatter any face shape.

4 **Change your hair color.** Adding highlights or switching shades is a surefire way to score a different look—minus the shears. The truly change-phobic can choose between wash-out-that-night hues, and semipermanent dyes that brighten or deepen your natural shade and fade out over the course of a few weeks. For a more dramatic dye job—like going from brown to blond, or adding lighter streaks—you'll need to use permanent hair color, which stays put until new hair starts to grow in.

5 **Pull it back.** The best way to see how you'll feel about having short hair is to try wearing your hair off your face. If you're not in love with the idea of exposing, say, your nose or your ears, this is a good way to find out.

6 **Change your part.** Okay, so it's the subtlest of changes. But it's also the most reversible. If you wear a center part, change it to a deep side part. If your part is ruler-straight, try a zigzag part.

7 **Accessorize.** Don't underestimate the power of hair accessories to rev up a dull 'do. Pair your new parting with a skinny, stretchy headband. Dangle dozens of jeweled barrettes from your romantic waves. Wrap your ponytail in a piece of suede or leather cord for instant hippie chic. The possibilities are endless, and the fun of mixing and matching different clips and bands with different outfits will help distract you from your hairstyle rut.

DID U KNOW? Hair grows slightly faster during the summer than in the winter, and tends to shed more rapidly during fall and spring.

QUIZ:
RED LIGHT/GREEN LIGHT

Psyched for a major change? Ready to chop off all your curls? Sounds like a cool idea, but you might want to consult your mood ring—and your calendar—first. Sure, change can be a good thing, but it can also be a not-so-good thing if you're making it for the wrong reasons or at the wrong time. Answer the following questions to find out if you're really ready for a new look.

1. Changing your hair is:
a) Your idea. You've had the same style since third grade and you're totally bored.
b) Your new boyfriend's idea. He thinks you'd look hotter with short hair.

2. You want a really killer new 'do for your senior prom, which just happens to be:
a) Tonight.
b) A month away.

3. You've been thinking about getting a trendy layered cut:
a) For weeks, ever since you tore out that magazine picture and stuck it to your mirror so you could get used to the idea.
b) Since homeroom this morning, when you saw your locker partner's cool new style.

4. On the way to your haircut appointment, you're feeling:
a) Pretty crabby. You failed the pop quiz, you caught your boyfriend flirting with that new French exchange student, and on top of everything, your period picked today to show up.
b) Pretty decent. Your planets must be aligned or something.

SCORING:

1. (a) green light
(b) red light
Go for a new look because you want it, not because a guy wants you to. Remember, the cut could last longer than the relationship.

2. (a) red light
(b) green light
It's a good idea to allow yourself plenty of time to get used to a new look (and learn how to style it) before a major photo-op like the prom, your Sweet Sixteen, etc. This is not a time to take a style risk from which there's no turning back.

3. (a) green light
(b) red light
Elvis was right when he sang "only fools rush in," especially when it comes to chopping off your locks. Unlike a new shade of eye shadow or nail polish, a new haircut can't exactly be wiped away if you don't like it. Consider any major metamorphosis for at least a few weeks before getting anywhere near the shears.

4. (a) red light
(b) green light
Contrary to popular belief, a makeover isn't always a cure for the blues. In fact, you're more likely to loathe any new look when you're feeling out of sorts (especially if you're experiencing the ever-popular PMS breakout the day of your haircut). Do yourself a favor and save the total makeover for a time when you're feeling less hormonally-challenged.

How To Get The Cut You Want

Ever sit in the stylist's chair, watching in silent horror as he or she turns the trim you asked for into spiky, ear-length layers? Or get talked into a bad perm that results in poodlelike locks? Now hear this: You don't have to be a Haircut Victim anymore! But you do have to speak up. The key to scoring a style you love is being able to explain what you want to your stylist. Here are a few points to consider:

- **Shopping for a stylist:** Looking for the right hairdresser? The best way to find one is by word of mouth. Ask anyone whose haircut you like who she goes to, even if she's a total stranger. *Another idea*: Ask a salon's manager to recommend a stylist who's an expert at cutting your type of hair.

- **Can we talk?:** Make sure the stylist takes time to consult with you about the style you want. Do this <u>before</u> your hair is shampooed, so that she/he has a chance to check out your hair type, texture, and any funky growth patterns. Don't be afraid to ask questions, like:
  - Is my hair texture and face shape right for the type of cut I want?
  - How much time will I have to spend styling this look?
  - What products and tools will I need?

  Now's the time for you to come clean about whether you're more the high-maintenance type or a wash-and-wear girl. A consultation is especially important if you're about to commit to a big change or you're seeing a brand-new stylist. If you're not comfortable with the stylist, visit another. Find someone you can bond with—not be intimidated by.

- **Picture perfect:** Look through magazines for ideas and inspiration. Bring your stylist a photo of the cut you crave. But be realistic: Try to choose pix of models or celebs who have the same hair type as yours, even the same hair color (that way, you'll be sure it's really the cut that caught your eye, not just that ravishing shade of red or platinum blond). If the 'do you're after isn't right for your hair or face shape, at least you and your stylist can use it as a starting point for discussion, and he or she can customize the cut to your hair's needs.

WORD OF ADVICE

If you're considering a major change, tape your dream haircut photo somewhere you can study it every day—like on your bathroom mirror or inside the door of your locker. Give yourself at least a week to mull it over—then, if you still want the cut, go for it.

- **Stop sign:** If you aren't happy with the way the cut is going, don't be afraid to ask the stylist to stop for a moment so you can air your fears. If you wait too long, it might be too late. Saying something like, "This isn't going to be too short, is it?" is a good way to break the ice if you're feeling freaked out about what you see in the mirror. A good stylist wants you to be happy—and come back.

- **Satisfaction guaranteed:** If you're less than thrilled with the results, resist the urge to keep it to yourself and sulk your way home. Share your concerns with your stylist, and be as specific as possible. She or he should tweak it until you're satisfied. If you're still not psyched—or the stylist is giving you a hard time—see the salon manager. He or she should offer to have someone else restyle your hair, or refund your money.

"The best way to battle frizzies is to take a fabric softener sheet and rub it lightly over your hair."

— KELLIE, Tennessee
seventeen reader

PRO TIP: *Sometimes it's best to give a cut time to adjust to its new length, which can take anywhere from two to three days to a couple of weeks. The reason: When hair is first cut, the ends are unnaturally blunt. In time, the blunt ends taper off, and your haircut will actually look better as it settles into a more natural shape.*

*"An easy way to look très chic and instantly pretty
when you're having a bad hair day:
Pull hair back into a bun,
leaving a few thin strands loose around your face.
Make tiny braids with the loose strands,
then pin them back."*

— ANDREA, California
seventeen reader

You Grow, Girl!

Growing out an old cut can make you feel like you're having an endless bad hair day. Follow these tips to make the transition more bearable:

- First, decide on the look you're going for—a one-length bob, long layers, or long with bangs. That way, your stylist can reshape your cut each time you get a trim.

- When you hit the salon, don't let your stylist go overboard with the scissors. You'll be getting nowhere fast if more than what's actually grown in is cut off. On the plus side, microtrims help eliminate split ends and prevent breakage, so hair grows in healthy and strong.

- Prepare to spend an extra five minutes each day styling your hair. It may take more effort than usual to get your locks to look good during the in-between stage.

- If you're trying to nix your bangs, get a cut that's gently angled around your face. It will make the difference between your bangs and the rest of your hair less noticeable. When growing-out fringe starts to hang in your eyes, try changing your part from one side to the other, or switching from a center to a side part. This helps create height and lifts your bangs up a bit. Eventually bangs will grow long enough to tuck behind your ears, and with a little help from a few bobby pins, they'll stay there.

- To even out shaggy layers, keep getting the ends trimmed straight across while allowing the top layers to grow out. After several trims, the top layers should begin to reach the bottom ones, giving hair a one-length look.

TIPS ON TIPPING

ALL STYLISTS EXPECT TO RECEIVE A TIP, AND OFTEN IT'S CONFUSING TO FIGURE OUT HOW MUCH CASH TO SLIP THEM. *SEVENTEEN* ASKED TOP STYLISTS AROUND THE COUNTRY FOR THEIR ADVICE:

If you're crazy about your new look, it's nice to give your stylist 15 to 20 percent of what the salon charges for the cut.

If the results are merely mediocre, 10 percent is adequate.

If you hate the cut, or the stylist was rude to you or didn't listen to your concerns, it's okay to withold a tip completely.

If someone other than the stylist shampooed or helped blow-dry your hair, you should tip him or her a dollar or two.

Feeling awkward about handing over the money? At most salons, the receptionist provides discreet little envelopes just for this purpose.

You love the way your bangs draw attention to your eyes or hide your wide forehead… but not the way they seem to grow so much faster than the rest of your cut. When your fringe starts flopping, hit the salon for a two-minute bang trim (most salons offer them for free as long as you call before coming in).

If you're feeling talented and want to trim your own bangs, try this tactic:

1 Dampen your bangs and pull them away from your head at a 90-degree angle.

2 Holding hair taut between your index and middle fingers, place small, straight-edged scissors directly behind your fingers and snip straight across.

3 Cut off a tiny bit at a time (say, an eighth of an inch), and be sure to leave bangs on the long side (wet hair can shrink up to an inch when it dries, even more if it's curly). Remember, you can always trim more…but you can't reverse the cut once it's done.

Unruly Bangs

Can't get your bangs under control?
Got a cowlick that wants to curl left when you want to style it right?
Here are some hints on taming freaky fringe:

• Style your bangs *before* you work on the rest of your hair. Wrap wet bangs around a medium-size round brush and blow-dry, pointing the dryer's nozzle straight down. Then, while your hair is still hot, place the brush (or your hand) on top of your bangs and gently flatten them against your forehead. To lock in the shape, let your hair cool this way.

• If you have a cowlick (an irregular pattern, usually at your hairline or crown, that causes strands to stand on end or grow in a different direction), apply a bit of styling gel at the root of it before you blow-dry.

• Sometimes an uneven hairline can cause problems with the way bangs hang. If this is the case, you need a cut that works with your hairline (this might involve longer bangs, brushing them to the side, or even growing them out).

BANG-UP JOB

*"If you have bangs, the oil from your hair
can make you break out on your forehead.
Try sleeping with a clip holding
your bangs away from your face.
It has really helped my complexion."*

— COLLEEN, Texas
seventeen reader

PRO TIP: *If you use a heated curling iron or straightening iron, smooth a bit of silcone-based shine serum on your hair first. The serum helps the iron glide through your hair, so your tresses are less likely to burn. Bonus: The heat helps seal in the shine.*

Love your 'do when you leave the salon, but hate it the next day? According to the top stylists we work with on **seventeen** photo shoots, the number-one cause of bad hair days is—surprise!—not having bad hair, but using the wrong styling tools (or using the right ones the wrong way). Learning which brush, blow-dryer, rollers, or iron is best for your style can be just as important as getting a great cut. Here's a guide to all the cool tools you'll need to perfect your look:

Brushes

Since the main purpose of your brush is styling, pick one that's the right size and shape to give your 'do the desired look:

- ## Round brushes
  - Use a **small round brush** for short hair, to add curl to the ends of longer hair, or to style bangs.
  - **Medium round brushes** (for shoulder-length hair) and **large round brushes** (for longer hair) are great for straightening wavy or curly hair during blow-drying, because their bristles grab locks and create the necessary tension. If you plan to use your round brush for straightening, go for one with natural, or mostly natural, bristles.
  - Hair should be long enough to wrap all the way around your round brush. *Warning:* Don't wrap hair around the brush multiple times while you're styling—it's likely to get caught in the bristles.
  - While most round brushes have wooden or plastic bases, some come with metal bases that trap heat from your dryer and work like hot rollers to lock a curl or wave in place.

- ## Half-round brushes

  Half-round brushes have more widely spaced bristles set in a rubber base. Use to add lift at the roots while blow-drying and for smoothing bangs. For extra styling control, pick one with nylon bristles.

- ## Flat brushes

  Flat brushes tend to have oval-shaped heads set in a rubber base. Look for one with a combination of natural bristles (for smoothing) and nylon (for styling control). Use to straighten slightly wavy hair while blow-drying or to smooth hair back into a ponytail or updo.

HEAD GEAR

- ## Paddle brushes

  Paddle brushes have large, flat, rectangular heads that make it easier to blow-dry large sections of long hair faster. Paddle brushes are ideal for straight or wavy hair. Because the bristles tend to be farther apart, they can't create enough tension to straighten curly hair.

- ## Vent brushes

  Vent brushes have widely spaced plastic bristles and holes in the base, so air from your dryer can flow through. Use to add lift at the roots and help dry your hair faster.

> Brushing your hair can help make it healthier, as long as you do it gently. A few strokes each night with a natural bristle brush revs up scalp circulation (encouraging growth) and helps distribute natural oils from your scalp to the ends of your hair. But more isn't always more: Vigorous brushing roughs up the hair's cuticle and can lead to breakage and split ends. Ditto when brushing wet hair—it's weaker and breaks more easily, so it's better to use a comb on waterlogged locks.

Combs

Who needs a comb if you've got the right styling brush? You, that's who. There's no better tool for detangling your locks, separating hair into sections for blow-drying, or grooming curly hair without adding to the frizz factor.

- **Wide-toothed combs** have teeth that are spaced far apart, so they can comb through towel-dried hair without snagging and breaking the hair.

- **Fine-toothed combs** are great for parting or sectioning hair (choose one with a long, pointed handle that can be used as a tool on its own), or teasing hair slightly at the roots to add volume.

- **Picks** have long, widely spaced teeth and are the tool of choice for arranging curly hair.

How do I keep my brushes and combs clean? How often do I need to buy a new brush?

See all that gnarly hair that builds up on your brush? Not only does it look gross, but the more it builds up, the less effective your brush will be. Remove the hair by combing through the bristles with a fine-toothed comb. Once a month or so, soak brushes and combs in hot water with a little shampoo or mild dish soap. (If your brush is made of wood, dip it quickly instead of soaking, so it doesn't warp.) Rinse the brush under clear water, and roll it in a towel to remove excess water. Then unroll and allow to air-dry. Replace brushes when bristles start to bend or break off.

Blow-dryers

Blow-dryer heat has the obvious benefit of drying your hair faster, but it also helps create a style (whether you're adding curl or straightening). Here's what to look for:

- **Multiple settings for heat and speed:** They allow you to control both how hot the air is and how powerfully it comes out. In general, a high setting is best for thick manes, medium for fine tresses, and low for delicate hair or scrunching natural curls.

- **High wattage:** Most dryers range from 1,200 to 1,875 watts. For best results, go for at least 1,500 watts (higher if you'll be using the dryer to straighten wavy or curly hair).

- **A cool-shot button:** Finishing a style with a blast of cold air helps seal it in place.

- **Attachments:**
  - A **nozzle** attachment helps concentrate air where you direct it (perfect for straightening).
  - A **diffuser** attachment softens the airflow so it doesn't bring on the frizzies when drying curly hair.
  - A **volumizing** attachment has teeth that help lift hair away from your roots as you dry it, creating maximum body. *Hot fact:* You can do the same maneuver with your fingers.

Curl Friends

Check out these wave-makers:

- **Curling iron:** When choosing a curling iron, remember the larger the barrel (the part you wrap your hair around), the looser the curl will be. If you like tight ringlets, try an iron with a half-inch barrel. To add body without curl, opt for a jumbo one-and-a-quarter-inch barrel. Want curls in a hurry? Look for a quick-heating iron (some heat up in as little as 60 seconds).

- **Heated rollers:** Like curling irons, heated rollers should be chosen based on the desired effect: Smaller rollers yield tighter, bouncier curls, and larger rollers add body and lift. Steam rollers add moisture to hair with a protective hot mist.

- **Velcro rollers**: If you want to minimize heat damage to your hair, go "unplugged" with Velcro rollers. The Velcro coating attaches to hair and holds the roller in place without clips. Use on damp hair and allow to air-dry completely, or direct heat from a blow-dryer at rollers to speed things up.

- **Hot air brush or curling brush:** This curling tool looks like a round brush with bristles, but it heats up (either with a blast of hot air, as a blow-dryer does, or through its metal base, like an iron). The bristles help grab hair and keep it wrapped around the brush.

Straighteners

Go sleek with these tress-flatteners:

- **Flattening or straightening irons:** If you love the stick-straight look, nothing beats a flattening iron—two large, flat panels that heat up and press sections of hair between them. Use on dry hair only.

- **Steam straightener:** If your hair is dry and delicate, try a straightening iron with built-in steam. The hot, damp air adds moisture to locks as it dekinks curls.

PRO TIP: *Don't feel the burn! Whether you're working with a curling iron, a straightening iron, or heated rollers, wait until your hair is dry. Not only is trying to heat-style wet or damp hair a waste of time, but the heat can cause the H_2O in your hair to sizzle and burn you!*

Gels, mousses, serums, and other style-savers help give your 'do shape and support, and come with varying levels of hold (the ratings are based on a scale of 0 to 5, with 0 being no hold and 5 being mega-hold). Here's a roundup of what each one does, and how to apply it for best results:

STYLING PRODUCTS

Product:	**Shine Serum or Mist**
HOLD FACTOR:	0
WHAT IT DOES:	Shine-boosting serums or mists contain silicone, an ingredient that makes hair glossy and silky and helps control frizz.
HOW TO USE IT:	Put a pea-size amount on your palms and rub them together to warm up the product (this thins it out into an even film all over your hands). Starting from the back of your head and working toward the front, run your hands lightly over damp hair in a downward direction to distribute the product. When hair is dry, up the shine factor by misting spray on lightly or smoothing on a tiny bit more serum.

Product:	**Styling Cream or Balm**
HOLD FACTOR:	1
WHAT IT DOES:	• Makes damp hair easier to detangle. • Adds a touchable, "piece-y" texture, without stiffness or stickiness. • Protects hair from heat styling. • Controls fuzzy fly-aways.
HOW TO USE IT:	Squeeze a dab onto your fingers, then rub them together. Beginning at your roots, work the cream or balm through wet or dry hair (using on dry hair creates more texture).

Product:	**Mousse**
HOLD FACTOR:	3
WHAT IT DOES:	Adds texture, body, and soft hold to fine, limp hair.
HOW TO USE IT:	Squirt a quarter-size dollop of foam onto your palm (use less for short hair). Dip the teeth of a comb into it and work it through wet hair from roots to ends.

Product:	**Straightening Balm**
HOLD FACTOR:	3
WHAT IT DOES:	Use with a round brush and heat from a blow-dryer to help make curly hair straight.
HOW TO USE IT:	Apply a quarter-size amount to damp, towel-dried hair and comb through from roots to ends to distribute evenly. Separate hair into sections and blow dry each one straight, pulling with a round brush as you dry.

Product:	**Gel**
HOLD FACTOR:	3-5 (depending on the formula)
WHAT IT DOES:	Gels come in different degrees of hold, from soft to superstrong, which usually leave a hard, wet-looking finish. A small dab adds volume and support at the roots. A larger amount can slick hair back for a wet look. Thinner, spray-on gels can also be used to control curls or add texture to layered looks.
HOW TO USE IT:	Place gel on wet hair. Massage into roots only if you want lift there. Spritz on spray gels and comb through with a wide-toothed comb for overall texture and hold.

Product: Volumizer

HOLD FACTOR:	3
WHAT IT DOES:	Volumizers come in spray and cream forms, and contain ingredients that swell and separate individual strands, so you look like you have more hair.
HOW TO USE IT:	Lift sections of damp, towel-dried hair and spritz on volumizing spray or work in volumizing cream at the roots before blow-drying. Avoid the ends (heavy sprays and creams tend to weigh them down too much).

Product: Wax or Pomade

HOLD FACTOR:	3-4 (depending on the formula)
WHAT IT DOES:	Creates definition and messy, tousled texture on shorter, layered styles, and adds a glossy shine without stiffness.
HOW TO USE IT:	Waxes and pomades work best when they're warmed up between your palms before you slick them on. For maximum texture, use on dry hair or on wet hair that you'll allow to air-dry. For a less edgy look, use on wet hair before blow-drying.

Product: Hairspray

HOLD FACTOR:	3-5 (depending on the formula)
WHAT IT DOES:	Holds a style in place and controls fly-aways.
HOW TO USE IT:	Pick your formula based on how much support your hair needs. Our favorites are the ultralight, flexible-hold versions that prevent that helmet-head look. Aerosols mist on more lightly and dry faster, so they're better for fine hair. Pumps go on a little gloopier and work better on thicker hair. Formulas with alcohol tend to dry faster, while alcohol-free ones take longer, but are better for dry, chemically treated hair.

BUILD-UP ALERT

At **seventeen**, we see many models come in for photo shoots with limp, dull-looking hair. What's with that? Like some of you, the models spritz and spray tons of styling products on their hair each week—and sometimes, those mousses, serums, and gels do their job a little too well. They attach themselves to your hair and resist your regular shampoo. To break the buildup cycle, try lathering up with a deep-cleansing clarifying shampoo once or twice a week. Baking soda can also do the job—just sprinkle some on damp hair and comb through. Let it sit for fifteen minutes, then rinse really well.

Dear seventeen:

Does changing shampoos all the time make your hair look better?

There's no scientific reason to switch shampoos unless your hair changes (that is, if you've colored or permed it, if winter weather is making it drier than usual, or if you've just joined the swim team). Once or twice a week, you may want to alternate in a formula that does a specific job (a clarifying shampoo to remove mineral and styling product buildup, or a color-enhancing shampoo to keep your shade bright). That said, if you find your hair looks and feels "fresher" when you change formulas frequently, by all means play the switching game. Maybe your hair knows something the chemists at shampoo companies don't.

Splitsville: What To Do About Split Ends

You're twirling a strand of your hair as your teacher reviews last night's assignment. You glance down and can't believe what you see! Your ends are frayed and split. How did this happen?

Split ends are caused by:

- Too much heat styling at too high a setting

- Vigorous brushing

- Exposure to sun and wind

- Too much time between trims

How do you fix it?

- Once ends fray, they tend to split. There's no way to really repair them besides trimming them off—so it's a good idea to **get a trim every six weeks.**

- To keep more splits from sprouting, use a natural bristle brush (it won't snag strands).

- Always condition after you shampoo. Once a month, use a deep conditioner.

- To mask split ends, work a dab of deep conditioner into damp hair before styling. Or try a split-end repair treatment designed to temporarily fuse forked locks. If your split ends do an antennaelike thing once your hair is dry, work in an anti-humectant pomade to control them and seal in moisture.

HAIR REPAIR

A SHINY IDEA

After shampooing and conditioning, rinse hair with icy-cold water to make hair look extra shiny. This will help smooth the cuticle (the microscopic, shingle-like outer coating of each strand), so it lies flat and is able to reflect the light.

STRAIGHT-FROM-THE-PANTRY SHINE BOOSTERS

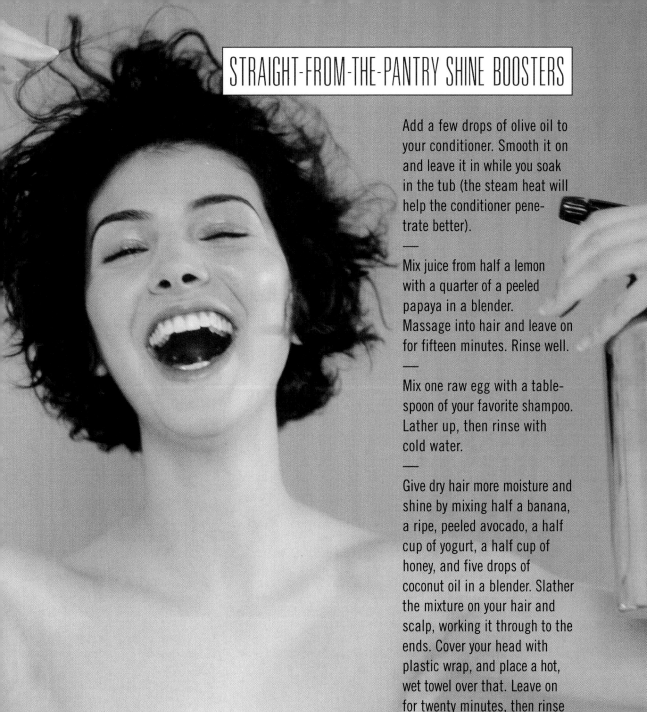

Add a few drops of olive oil to your conditioner. Smooth it on and leave it in while you soak in the tub (the steam heat will help the conditioner penetrate better).

—

Mix juice from half a lemon with a quarter of a peeled papaya in a blender. Massage into hair and leave on for fifteen minutes. Rinse well.

—

Mix one raw egg with a tablespoon of your favorite shampoo. Lather up, then rinse with cold water.

—

Give dry hair more moisture and shine by mixing half a banana, a ripe, peeled avocado, a half cup of yogurt, a half cup of honey, and five drops of coconut oil in a blender. Slather the mixture on your hair and scalp, working it through to the ends. Cover your head with plastic wrap, and place a hot, wet towel over that. Leave on for twenty minutes, then rinse out and wash hair with a moisturizing shampoo.

Do the math: It means a full-length hair would grow as long as eighteen to thirty inches before falling out (that is, if you didn't cut it first).

DID U KNOW? Hair grows about a half-inch a month, and has an average growth cycle of three to five years.

She's Such A Flake

No one likes having an **itchy, flaky scalp.** Although **dandruff** is the number-one cause of this need-to-scratch condition, residue from strong-hold gel and dry, cold weather are also culprits.

Before you can fix it, you need to determine what is causing your itchy, flaky scalp:

- If your hair and skin are oily, any flaking you see could be dandruff. Dead skin cells shed at an accelerated rate due to hormonal changes. These changes weaken your scalp's normal resistance to dandruff-causing bacteria. Alternate your regular shampoo with a dandruff shampoo and see if the flakes clear up.

- If you use lots of styling gel, the flakes could be dried-up gel residue. Try skipping the gel for a few days to see if the situation improves. In the meantime, test to see if your gel dries flaky and opaque by putting some on a mirror and waiting for it to dry. If it doesn't dry clear, switch to another brand.

- Finally, the itchiness and dryness could be weather-related, especially if it's cold and dry outside and you're exposed to indoor heating. Try using a humidifier when you sleep at night, and slather on moisturizing conditioner each time you shampoo.

TEN LITTLE THINGS YOU CAN DO IN THE SHOWER THAT MAKE A BIG DIFFERENCE TO YOUR HAIR

1. When you shampoo, lather up twice. The first washing removes oil, dirt, and styling product buildup. The second helps add volume.

2. If your shampoo doesn't lather, your hair probably isn't wet enough. Try adding more water instead of more suds.

3. Don't pile your hair on top of your head when you're sudsing up—it can cause tangles.

4. If your hair is very dry, don't shampoo daily. Every other day, just wet hair while showering, apply conditioner, and rinse.

5. Wash your hair in warm water. If the water is too hot, it can make your scalp dry and itchy. If it's too cold, the shampoo may not rinse out thoroughly.

6. When you're in a rush, spot-shampoo your hair (for example, wash only your bangs or the area around your hairline).

7. Make sure you're using the right kind of conditioner: Protein-based ones help build strength and body. Moisturizing ones add softness and shine.

8. Before using conditioner, blot your hair with a towel, or at least squeeze out the excess water. When hair is waterlogged, conditioner can't be absorbed as effectively.

9. Apply conditioner to the midsection and the ends of your hair, not the roots.

10. Comb conditioner through wet hair with a wide-toothed comb to help distribute it evenly.

How do you avoid bed head?

No one would mind bed head if it looked like the tousled, sexy locks in the Victoria's Secret catalog. Unfortunately, garden variety bed head is decidedly less appealing: flat on one side and standing straight up on the other, or just one big tangled mess. If your schedule demands that you wash your hair at night instead of in the morning, remember that the damper your hair is when you hit the sack, the less predictable the results will be when you wake up. If possible, dry and style your hair completely the night before. To prevent tangle trouble, pull long hair up into a loose ponytail on top of your head before going to sleep (secure with a large scrunchie instead of an elastic to avoid a dent when you take out your ponytail in the morning). Another way to dodge snarls: Sleep on a satin pillowcase (it cuts down on friction).

Broken Hairs

What causes broken hairs:

- Making ponytails too tight
- Yanking out hair accessories
- Combing or brushing wet hair
- Using the wrong brush

How to fix them:

- Condition your hair after each shampoo, and apply a deep conditioner once a week to moisturize and strengthen brittle hair.

- Try not to comb or brush wet hair—it's more delicate and prone to breakage.

- When you pull hair back in a ponytail or barrettes, gather it gently and don't make it too tight. Always used covered elastic bands and look for barrettes and headbands without sharp teeth. Be extra gentle when removing any hair accessories.

- If you use a round brush for styling, keep it gliding through your locks (if you roll the brush up in your hair, it can get stuck and lead to breakage when you try to remove it).

- Minimize the appearance of broken hairs by spritzing a natural-bristle brush with hairspray and smoothing it over the wispy area.

Losing It

Noticing more hairs clogging up the shower drain lately? Relax—chances are you're not going bald. The increased fall-out rate is probably due to: a) chemical or heat-styling damage that's weakening your hair and causing it to break off, or b) your hair's normal molting phase.

To get to the root of the problem, find a fallen strand of hair and look for a bulb at one end. If there's no bulb, your hair is probably breaking off. If so, condition regularly and go easy on the heat styling and chemical treatments.

If you do see the bulb, don't freak: It's totally normal to shed about fifty to a hundred hairs per day, and up to twice as much during the spring and fall.

Gently massage your scalp with your fingertips (it stimulates blood flow, which encourages hair growth). Don't wear hair in too-tight ponytails or braids, and use covered elastics. If you're still losing a lot of strands in a few months, see your doctor to rule out other causes.

ALL TANGLED UP

WHAT CAUSES TANGLES?
Fine and very curly hair are more prone to tangles. Too-rough towel-drying can really knot up your mane. And a windy day is sure to twist up your tresses.

WHAT TO DO?
- Before shampooing, use a paddle brush on dry hair. Condition after shampooing, combing the conditioner through wet hair before rinsing out. Gently blot excess water out of hair with a towel, being careful not to rub or scrunch up hair.

- After towel-drying your wet hair, comb through with a wide-toothed comb. Start with the ends, then detangle the midsection, and finish by combing from the roots to the ends. Hold sections with your hands just above where you're combing to keep the comb from putting too much tension on wet hair.

- Protect long hair from the elements by wearing it in a braid or bun when you plan to be on the beach or the slopes.

I have combination hair—oily at the roots and really dry at the ends. What should I do?

When you shampoo, concentrate the suds on your scalp, not the ends of your hair. Alternatively, apply conditioner only to the ends of your locks, avoiding the roots. If your roots look really oily midday, try sprinkling on a bit of dry shampoo (a powdery substance that soaks up excess oil) or baby powder if you're a blond (powder tends to look noticeably chalky on darker hair). Brush it through, then mist the ends of your hair with a leave-in conditioner.

Fun In The Sun

You're playing volleyball on the beach, working as a lifeguard at the local pool, or just hanging out in your backyard. The humidity is, like, 200 percent, and you're in and out of the way-chlorinated pool or the salty ocean twelve times a day. With each activity, your hair is getting drier and frizzier, and you're getting more split ends. Here are some suggestions from the top sytlists that we've worked with to make summer hair gorgeous hair.

Sun exposure weakens hair's protein structure and causes it to lose its natural moisture. To make matters worse, both salt water and pool water do a drying number of their own on your locks. So before hitting the beach (or catching rays anywhere), comb a conditioner with built-in sunscreen into your locks. If you have long hair, braid it or twist it up in little "knots"—this way, fewer strands are exposed to the sun. Carry conditioner in your bag and slick some on when hair starts to feel dry.

It isn't easy being green

If you're a natural blond or have chemically lightened hair, pool water can cause your blond locks to turn green. The culprits behind the yucky greenish tinge are the copper and other minerals in the water.

Protect your color by wetting hair first with tap water or a spray bottle filled with seltzer, which counteracts the color-corroding pH level of pool water. Slick on some conditioner before taking the plunge. Conditioner will protect your hair from soaking up pool water. Even if it looks less than glam, it's best to wear a swim cap each time you take a dip. When you get out, rinse your hair with tap water and shampoo as soon as you get home. Once a week, alternate your regular shampoo with a deep-cleaning, detoxifying shampoo designed to remove mineral buildup, and condition regularly to counteract dryness.

PRO TIP: *Do-It-Yourself Conditioner: Fix summer-fried hair by mixing half an avocado with two ounces of plain yogurt. Slather it on your hair and leave it on for twenty minutes, then rinse.*

Yikes! My hair is orange!

Unprotected exposure to sun and salt water can cause color-treated hair to morph into a whole new (and usually undesirable) bright orange shade.

If you've plunked down a lot of money for professional highlights or color, it makes sense to protect your precious investment. When you hit the beach or play outdoor sports, cover up with a hat. Otherwise, be sure to protect your hair with a styling product with built-in sunscreen, like a light, spray-on, leave-in conditioner.

The Deep Freeze

Brrr...it's cold outside. Time for snowball fights, hot chocolate, and hitting the slopes! But between hair-raising static and limp, hat-flattened locks, your 'do can be somewhat style-challenged during cold weather.

Static electricity is caused when cold, dry air teams up with friction (as in putting on and taking off your hat or wool sweater, or brushing your hair). This sets off an electrical charge that makes strands stand on end.

To prevent static stick-up, try shampooing only every other day, and condition, condition, condition. The more you hydrate your hair, the calmer it will be. Avoid styling products that contain drying alcohol. Tame out-there hair by spritzing a leave-in conditioner on a natural-bristle brush and running it through your locks. *Another fast fix:* Raid the laundry room and spray a little Static Guard on your hands, then run them lightly over your hair.

Hat head. Need a definition? It's when your hair gets flattened by pulling a ski cap over it.

Fight the flatness by shampooing with body-enhancing shampoos and using lightweight detanglers instead of heavy conditioners. To avoid hat head, try not to pull your snug-fitting ski cap over wet hair in the morning rush—the drier your style is before you flatten it with your hat, the better the chance it has of springing back when you reach homeroom. Or trade your hat for a pair of toasty (and more hair-friendly) earmuffs.

"Add volume to flat hair by flipping your head over and blow-drying the bottom layers first. Next, spray the underlayers with hairspray, then flip your head back up and dry the top layers last."

— ANNIE, Texas
seventeen reader

Perms And Relaxers

No matter how well you've nailed your styling technique of choice, the results last only until your next shampoo. If you find yourself spending more time with your blow-dryer than your boyfriend, it might be time to consider a longer-lasting style-helper. Here's a roundup of what's out there:

Texturizing perms

What you want: Perfect waves every day.

What to ask for: A soft, texturizing permanent wave.

What to know: Don't let the word "perm" scare you. The current crop of chemical curling treatments produces natural-looking results.

How it works: You and your stylist decide on the type of curl you want, whether it's corkscrews or loose waves. The stylist wraps hair around the appropriate-size perm rod (the smaller the rod, the tighter the curl). Then the stylist applies the chemical solution, which is left on for ten to twenty minutes. Reperm after three to eight months, depending on how fast your hair grows and how much the straight regrowth bothers you.

When to skip it: If your hair has a lot of highlights or is bleached, it's the same old problem: Too many chemical processes at once can turn your strands into straw.

Volumizers

What you want: Extra-full hair, more lift at the roots.

What to ask for: A root-boosting volumizing treatment.

What to know: Once the only way to add volume to flat hair was to perm it at the roots, which added lift where it was most needed. The problem: As the perm grew out, you were left with a gradually descending kink or wave in your hair. But now a process called volumizing (or amplifying) promises fuller hair without the long-term commitment of most perms.

How it works: Your hair is sectioned and wrapped around large rollers. The volumizing solution is applied to your hair, left on for ten or twenty minutes, then rinsed out. A second chemical is then applied to the hair to lock in the look (the entire process takes less than an hour). Unlike a perm, a volumizing treatment lasts only about eight weeks, at which point the hair gradually reverts back to its natural texture.

When to skip it: If your hair is longer than shoulder length, it's probably too heavy to benefit from the root-lifting action.

TOTAL RECURL: PROTECTING YOUR PERM

Most perms need to set for a day or so to lock in the curl, so don't shampoo or use conditioner for at least 24 hours after perming (it is okay to wet hair and use styling products). Since any chemical treatment can rob hair of moisture, switch to a moisturizing shampoo made for chemically treated hair. Follow with a lightweight leave-in conditioner that won't weigh down curls (look for one without waxes or mineral oil). Wake up tired waves with a curl activator, a leave-in styling spray designed especially for curly or permed hair. If you blow-dry, protect curls with a diffuser attachment. At least once a week, saturate hair with a deep-conditioning protein pack or hot oil treatment.

Straighteners/relaxers

What you want: A break from the daily onslaught of trying to blow-dry and iron your hair straight.

What to ask for: A chemical straightening treatment (if your hair is slightly wavy to medium curly) or a relaxer (if your hair is coarse and very curly).

What to know: Until recently, straighteners and relaxers contained harsh, heavy ingredients like lye. Today's formulas are much kinder and gentler to your hair. Rather than making your hair poker-straight (not to mention brittle), they leave some of your hair's natural body intact. This allows you to choose between wearing it slightly wavy or easily styling it straight.

How it works: Both the straightener's formula (mild, regular, or super-strength) and the length of time it stays on the hair determine the final results, which can range from nearly straight to simply looser curls. The straightening solution is combed in evenly from the roots to the ends of your hair, left on for the prescribed amount of time, then rinsed out. Next, a neutralizer is applied to seal in the straightness. Relaxed hair stays straight until the roots grow in curly again.

When to skip it: If your hair is bleached, highlighted, or dyed, proceed with caution. Ask your colorist about special relaxers made for color-treated hair.

"Use body lotion as an anti-frizz product. Just put a nickel-size amount in the palm of your hand, rub hands together to distribute evenly, and smooth over your hair. It weighs it down enough to keep your 'do frizz-free, but doesn't look greasy."

— JENNIFER, California
seventeen reader

DOING IT YOURSELF

Perms and relaxers are also available in do-it-yourself home kits. They're more affordable than salon services, but they come with a price of their own: the risk of seriously screwing up your hair. First, it's important to choose the right formula for your hair type and the desired results. Follow directions very carefully, especially with regard to how long to leave the chemicals on your hair. (Most boxes are printed with the hair-care company's toll-free hot line in case you have questions—don't be afraid to use it!) If you're doing a home perm, remember that the size and placement of the rods dictates how curls will look.

Braids And Extensions

Braids and extensions give shorter hair an instant long look. Both are popular for African-American hair, but can be worn by all hair types.

Braids

Different types:

- **Casamance braids** are thick and flat.
- **Senegalese twists** and **corkscrews** look like rope.
- **Microbraids** are the skinniest.

How it's done: Your own hair is braided from the roots, then lengths of synthetic hair (it holds tightly braided styles better than human hair) are woven in.

How long it takes: It takes six to eight hours, average.

How long it lasts: Once they're on your head, braids can stay put for two to three months (though after about six weeks you'll need to go to the salon for maintenance—removing the braids around the hairline and replacing them with freshly done braids).

Pro tips: To keep your braids in shape while you sleep, wrap them in a silky scarf before you hit the pillow. Keep them shiny and conditioned with a **braid sheen mist.**

Extensions

Different types: Extensions, weaving, bonding.

How it's done:

- With **extensions**, your own hair is braided at the scalp, then individual lengths of hair (human or synthetic) are braided or sewn into your braids.
- With **weaving**, your hair is cornrowed into a network of interlocking braids, then a row or weft of already attached extensions is sewn on (this creates a bit more volume on top).
- **Bonding** is done with special glue and is generally thought to be more damaging to hair.

How long it takes: Extensions can take anywhere from a few hours to a whole day!

How long it lasts: Between three and four months (if you wait any longer, your own hair can mat and become very difficult to untangle).

Pro tips: Be gentle when you're combing, brushing, and shampooing.

HAIR, THERE, AND EVERYWHERE

KEEP THESE STYLING ESSENTIALS IN YOUR BAG:

- A purse-size version of your favorite brush (an oval brush is great for midday styling touch-ups or smoothing hair back into a ponytail).

- A silicone shine serum or mist (rub a bit on your palms and smooth over your 'do to nix frizzies).

- An assortment of barrettes and covered elastics for keeping long hair under control.

Special-occasion Looks

Proms, parties, anywhere your crush is going to be: No matter what the occasion (or whom you're trying to impress), there are times when you'll want to try something special with your hair. Here's what to do if you want to...

Give your straight hair smooth spiral curls:

1. Spritz a volumizing spray on your roots.

2. Lift hair at the roots and scrunch while blow-drying with a diffuser attachment to encourage waves.

3. When your hair is completely dry, separate it into small sections with clips. Curl each section with a curling iron (remember, the smaller the iron's barrel, the tighter the curls will be). For best results, hold the iron vertically and grab the middle of a section of hair in its clamp first. Next, wrap the loose ends of the section around the iron, then roll the iron up to your roots. Hold for a few seconds, then release and allow each new curl to air-cool completely before touching it.

4. When you're finished curling sections, arrange curls with your fingers or a pick (brushing pulls out the curl) and mist with a soft-hold flexible hairspray.

Create a romantic updo:

Updos can be sleek, spiky, or softly tousled and worn high at the crown or low at the nape of your neck. First, decide whether you look best with a part (center, off center, diagonal, zigzag—whatever) or with hair pulled straight back off your forehead. If you have bangs or face-framing layers, leave them loose.

- To create a cool topknot, gather the rest of your hair high at the crown and secure with an elastic band. Twist the ponytail and allow it to coil around the base of the ponytail, securing with pins against your head as you coil it.

- For a sleek French twist, gather your hair low at the nape of your neck, then start twisting it up tightly against the back of your head, pinning it at the crown. Traditional twists get the ends tucked in, but look prettier if you leave a few inches loose at the ends.

- To loosen up either look even more, pull out some pieces around your face. Mist your 'do with hairspray all over to give it staying power. *Dirty little secret:* Any kind of updo, from a topknot to a French twist, holds better on slightly dirty (last-shampooed yesterday) hair.

Get instant long locks:

For a truly big event, you might want to invest in a hairpiece—a length of real or synthetic hair that comes in the form of a fall or a ponytail. A fall gets attached like a headband to the top of your head, behind your ears. You can buy these do-it-yourself extensions at wig shops or beauty supply stores. For a natural, believable look, try to match your faux hair to the color of your real locks. For a more dramatic I'm-wearing-fake-hair-and-I-don't-care-who-knows-it look, go for a contrasting shade (they even come in pastels to match your prom dress or your nail polish).

- **How to use a fall:** Smooth your own hair back and pin it behind your ears with flat bobby pins. Then attach the fall to the crown of your head with stronger hairpins—most falls come with combs or loops inside for this purpose.

- **To attach a faux ponytail:** Gather your own hair back into a ponytail (if it's long enough) or bun. Pin on the fake hair just above your own ponytail or bun. Secure it tightly with at least four hairpins to guarantee that your tail won't get left behind on the dance floor!

Everything You Need To Know About Hair Color

Nothing changes your look more dramatically than changing your hair color. Need proof? Look at the way golden-girl actresses seem to turn dark and mysterious when they go brunette for a movie role or how your favorite music-video stars morph from glam platinum blond to funky Technicolor fuchsia with each new album.

Not into playing the color chameleon yourself? Try a subtler change by brightening up your locks with some head-turning highlights or a no-commitment color gloss. Whether you want to radically change your color or just enhance your natural hue, check out this guide to doing the dye thing:

WHAT YOU WANT: TO ROAD-TEST A NEW HUE JUST FOR ONE NIGHT.

HOW TO GET IT: With a temporary color (they come in cream, rinse, gel, pomade, spray, or hair mascara formulas) that shampoos right out.

HOW LONG IT LASTS: It doesn't—that's the beauty of it.

BONUS: It's zero-commitment color that can look as natural (add faux blond or copper highlights) or supernatural (go for fierce purple streaks) as you want.

BUMMER: Your rainbow streaks could come off on your pillowcase, your collar, your boyfriend's hands— you get the picture. And the texture of color created by thick creams and mascaras can be a little sticky and stiff-looking.

PRO TIPS: Since sprays, pomades, and gels can be goopy and sticky, they're best used selectively rather than all over. If you have a short cut, try painting just the ends of your hair. For bangs, apply color to the fringe, then brush to blend (don't forget to wash your brush). Layer one cool hue on top of another for a more intense look. If you're streaking your long locks with hair mascara, coat the entire wand instead of the tip.

WHAT YOU WANT: AN ALLOVER BOOST OF BOLDER, BRIGHTER, OR DEEPER COLOR; MAJOR SHINE.

HOW TO GET IT: With a semi- or demipermanent dye.

HOW LONG IT LASTS: Semipermanent color lasts about six to twelve shampoos. Demipermanent shades last about twenty-four to twenty-eight shampoos.

BONUS: Stronger pigments mean these products last longer than temporary ones, but since they don't contain peroxide, they fade out gradually, so you never see any roots. Because they don't penetrate hair very deeply, they leave it in healthy shape. *Another plus:* Superconditioning ingredients give locks tons of added gloss.

BUMMER: Both kinds of dyes contain little or no ammonia, so they can't make your natural hair color lighter—only brighter or deeper.

PRO TIPS: If you start out with light hair, beware: Darker tones may stain your hair longer than the few weeks they're supposed to last. Not sure if your hair will soak up too much color? Try this test: Dampen a section and coat it with conditioner. Wait one minute, then run your fingers down the strand. If the conditioner seems to have soaked into some areas but feels slippery in others, hair is probably too damaged to take color evenly.

WHAT YOU WANT: TO GO A LOT LIGHTER, REDDER, OR DARKER.

HOW TO GET IT: With permanent hair color, which uses ammonia and peroxide to penetrate the hair, lift its natural pigment, and deposit new color on top.

HOW LONG IT LASTS: Until it grows out.

BONUS: Permanent color is the only kind that allows you to pull a total switcheroo. Because it penetrates the hair shaft and alters hair's structure, it can also make fine hair feel and look thicker.

BUMMER: Majorly noticeable roots. Hair grows about half an inch a month, so depending on how different your new hue is from your own color, you probably won't be fooling anyone for too long. Also, repeated lightening can dry out your hair.

PRO TIPS: At-home permanent dyes are designed to lighten or darken your natural hair's hue two to four shades. For drastic changes (say, turning black hair platinum blond), head for the salon. If your hair is newly relaxed or permed, wait a week before using any permanent color—your hair's already fragile state could cause it to snap from too many chemical processes. (If in doubt, consult a professional before applying dye.)

WHAT YOU WANT: MULTIDIMENSIONAL STREAKS OF COLOR.

HOW TO GET IT: With highlights—permanent color painted onto select pieces of hair instead of all over.

HOW LONG IT LASTS: Like all-over permanent color, highlights grow out. Because highlights are only added to certain random strands, roots tend to be less noticeable as they grow in.

BONUS: You—or your colorist—control how subtle or intense the effect is. A couple of face-framing streaks can make you look like you've been spending lots of time outdoors, while a whole head of highlights can totally change your hair color.

BUMMER: If you plan on layering a semipermanent color on top of your highlights, look out: Lightened hair absorbs color superfast and stains easily, meaning that the semipermanent hue may take more and last longer on the highlighted pieces.

PRO TIPS: At-home highlighting kits work best on hair that's naturally light brown or lighter. Dark-haired girls can easily end up with brassy stripes instead of the tortoiseshell look they were going for, so it's best to go to a salon if you want the job done right.

Making Color Last

Follow these tips to give your new hair color more staying power:

- **Shampoo less often.** Sudsing up too frequently can strip hair of natural oils, which leads to dull color. Instead, once or twice a week, rinse your hair with plain old H_2O, and massage your scalp to distribute those oils.

- When you do lather up, **go for shampoo and conditioner formulas made for color-treated hair** (they use low-detergent cleansers designed to leave color intact, plus built-in moisturizers to counteract dryness).

- To keep your new hue bright in between dye jobs, use a **color-enhancing shampoo** once or twice a week. These tinted washes come in a slew of colors and deposit a tiny amount of pigment each time you shampoo.

- Whenever possible, **go unplugged.** Blow-drying and other heat styling can suck shine-boosting moisture out of your hair.

- If you use styling products, choose **alcohol-free** formulas. Alcohol can dry out already dry colored hair even more.

- When you're going outside, **protect your color from sun-induced fading** by covering up with a hat or bandanna, or at least using a styling product with built-in **sunscreen**. Be especially careful if your new hue is red—auburn hues tend to fade fastest.

Lightening Lingo:
A Hair Color Glossary

Baliage: Technique in which highlights are painted on freehand with a brush.

Bleach: Removes pigment from hair—the only way for brunettes to go light blonde.

Demipermanent color: Ammonia-free, low-peroxide dye that can enhance or brighten (not lighten) a shade. Lasts about 24 to 28 shampoos before gradually fading away.

Double-process: Lightening your hair color all over, then depositing another tone—or highlights—on top of it.

Foils: A highlighting technique in which little squares of aluminum foil are used to separate strands that will be made lighter than the rest of hair.

Gloss: A conditioning, shine-enhancing treatment that fills in damaged areas of hair, creating a smooth, light-reflecting surface. Gloss formulas come in tints that can brighten or deepen color, or clear (for a shine boost with no color change).

Henna: Natural, plant-based dye that can deepen or brighten your hair without using peroxide or ammonia.

Highlights: Lightening certain strands or streaks with permanent color instead of lightening all over.

Lowlights: The opposite of highlights; darker tones are added to select strands of hair to make your natural shade appear brighter. Best for brunettes or dark redheads, or for correcting color overload.

Permanent color: Dye that lightens or deposits color using ammonia to penetrate the hair shaft. It's the only way, besides bleaching, to lighten hair. The new hue lasts until it grows out.

Semipermanent color: Like demipermanent color, except it lasts for a shorter time (about six to twelve shampoos) before gradually fading away.

Single-process: Getting all-over color (either semipermanent, demipermanent, or permanent) instead of highlights.

Temporary color: Ammonia- and peroxide-free dye that coats the hair temporarily and shampoos right out.

Vegetable dye: Plant-based color like henna.

Choosing A Colorist

Checking out a color pro and his or her salon is just as essential as taking a new car for a test drive. Here are a few things to look for:

- Natural daylight (or at least halogen lighting) in the color area. If the lighting is dull and yellow, your color will probably look the same way.

- Free consultations. Getting color is a complicated process, so the colorist should take the time to explain what it will take (and what it will cost) to achieve the look you want.

- A colorist who gives you the third degree (about your hair, that is). If he or she doesn't ask you whether you've had a chemical process within the last two years, it's almost the same as a doctor not asking you if you're allergic to anything before prescribing medication.

DID U KNOW? Colored powders (made from flour and tinted with crushed gold dust) were among the earliest

styling products. They were used to tint hair or, in the case of eighteenth-century French courtesans, added to elaborate white wigs.

Homegrown Highlights

Do you want to experiment with coloring your hair, but you're not ready to commit to a major color overhaul? Just raid your fridge. That's right—certain kitchen ingredients have a rep for revving up your hair color. These natural highlights won't change you from a brunette to a blonde, but they will intensify the color you already have. *Warning:* If your hair is very light blond, chemically treated, or damaged, skip the following recipes. Stuff like berries and coffee can stain pale and/or porous hair a little more permanently than you'd like. Also, wear an old T-shirt or towel when you apply ingredients—they can stain your clothes, too!

Blondes and light brunettes:

- Steep a **chamomile tea bag** in half a cup of hot water. When it cools, use the wet bag like a sponge and run it over your hair. Mixed with sunlight, chamomile can give hair a gleaming golden lift that lasts until hair grows out.

- Try saturating wet hair with **lemon juice**. Fill a spray bottle with about half a cup (more for longer hair) of lemon juice. Spritz it on the area around your hairline, then comb through and let the sun do the rest. For a more dramatic effect, apply juice to dry hair. (Keep in mind that acidic citrus can be drying, so be sure to condition lemon-lightened hair regularly.)

Light to dark brown hair:

- **Cranberries** can help bring out auburn highlights in light to dark brown shades. Mash half a pound of boiled cranberries into a paste, and mix in one teaspoon of **wheat-germ oil** (available in health-food stores). Comb the paste through wet hair, and wrap your head in a hot, wet towel (no need for sun exposure with this one). Leave on for twenty minutes, then rinse.

- To add richness and shine to dark brown or black hair, brew a pot of **coffee** and collect the grinds left over in the filter. Mix them with one teaspoon of **wheat-germ oil** and two tablespoons of **plain yogurt**. Massage into wet hair, leave on for twenty minutes, then rinse.

- Because berries and coffee coat only hair's outer layer with color, their brightening effects are temporary.

Black hair:

- To play up hair's natural blue-black luminescence, mash a half-pint of **blueberries** and slather the paste onto your hair. Cover with a shower cap for twenty minutes, then rinse thoroughly.

"Add some gleam to dull hair by mixing some sparkles into your hair gel and working it into your hair."

— KRISTEN, Washington
seventeen reader

Hair Cheat Sheet

Ready for a quick recap?
Here are the crucial points to remember when
it comes to getting great hair:

- When shopping around for a new style, look for one that will suit both your hair type and your face shape.

- Get the cut you want by bringing in pictures from magazines of the styles you like. Don't be afraid to speak up if the stylist starts doing something you're not happy with.

- Fight off bad hair days by choosing the right tools and styling products for your hair. Learn how to use them properly. Ask your stylist for a crash course before leaving the salon.

- Treat your hair like your favorite cashmere sweater—gently. Limit heat-styling and overbrushing.

- Minimize frizz by keeping your hands (and your brush or comb) off of curly hair while it's drying.

- Protect your hair color from the sun, seawater, and pool water by covering up with a hat or swim cap and conditioning regularly.

- Have fun experimenting with color, but be smart about it. If you want to make a radical color change, get advice from a pro before attempting it yourself.

chapter 3

SKIN CARE

Skin Magic

I f the Beauty Genie promised to grant us just one wish, most people would have no trouble deciding what it would be. We'd swap a year of good hair days or perfectly applied makeup for smooth, flawless skin—you know, the kind with even tone, microscopic pores, and no zits.

First the bad news: Close encounters with the Beauty Genie are about as common as bumping into Santa Claus or the Easter Bunny. Now the good news: **You don't need magic to get glowing, gorgeous skin.** What you do need is a skin-care plan designed to address your complexion's unique needs, whether we're talking breakouts, excess shine, or dryness. Over the years, **seventeen** picked the brains of dozens of dermatologists, hit up hundreds of models and celebs for their skin-care secrets, and personally road-tested thousands of cleansers, lotions, and potions. And everything we've learned (everything useful, that is) is right here in this chapter.

How to Get Great Skin...

Okay, so now on to the big question: **How do you get great skin?**

First, it's important to look at what causes skin woes. Some skin problems are simply genetic *(thanks, Mom and Dad)*. While these can't necessarily be prevented, you can learn how to treat them so their evidence is less...well... evident, on your face. Other skin problems are caused—or worsened—by environmental factors (like catching rays) and just plain bad skin-care habits. Chances are, you'll see an improved epidermis (that's dermologist-speak for skin) if you switch to a smarter strategy. The first step toward keeping your skin its healthiest is to determine your skin type—and the best way to care for it.

What's Your Skin Type?

Most people have some idea of which general category their skin falls into. The confusion comes when your skin starts to change. Skin-type changes are often due to internal factors like stress and hormonal swings (hello, puberty!), or even external factors like the weather. Your safest bet: Treat your skin based on how it's acting *right now*. Check out the chart below for clues on recognizing your skin's special needs.

Oily

How to recognize it: Your skin is seriously shiny before you wash your face in the morning, and by lunchtime, it's oily again. Skin is slick in the **T-zone** (forehead, nose, and chin), but it's usually oily around your hairline and cheeks, too. Your pores may appear enlarged. Pore size is predetermined by genes, but the openings can seem more noticeable when they're jammed with dead skin cells and excess oil.

How to cleanse it: Max out on sudsing twice a day (morning and bedtime), once more if you exercise. Lathering up more frequently can strip away too much of your skin's natural oils. That can cause irritation and maybe even send oil glands into overdrive to compensate for the dryness. Pick an **oil-free gel cleanser** containing the pore-declogging ingredient **salicylic acid.**

How to moisturize: If your skin is very oily, skip moisturizing.

How to troubleshoot:
- Soak up shine with an astringent—the alcohol in it penetrates your pores and evaporates oil. Or try a **mattefier**, a sheer, oil-absorbing lotion that can be worn alone or under makeup.
- For grease control plus coverage, try an **oil-free, oil-controlling foundation.** For a sheer finish, smooth foundation on with a moistened makeup sponge.
- Dust on loose powder instead of pressed. Pressed powders contain more oils, and the pressing action can clog pores.
- For midday touch-ups, carry a pack of tissue-thin blotting papers (they soak up oil and leave a featherweight matte finish behind). Presoaked astringent pads offer the same results, but keep in mind that they'll swipe off makeup at the same time.
- Once a week, try a **clay-based mask** to help give grease the slip.

"If you're at the mall and you've got a shiny face, blot the excess oil off with the toilet-seat cover paper in the ladies' room. It does the same thing as those blotting papers, and even better, it's free!"

— TIFFANY, California
seventeen reader

SKIN SAVVY

Acne-prone

How to recognize it: You have clogged pores that have morphed into **comedones** (blackheads or white-heads) and—if they become inflamed—**zits.** Though acne-prone skin tends to be oily, breakouts can also plague combination and even dry skin.

How to cleanse it: Gently—acne-prone skin tends to be irritated skin. In the morning and at bedtime, use a **nonsoap cleanser** with built-in acne-fighting ingredients like **salicylic acid** or **antibacterial benzoyl peroxide** (unless you find it makes your skin too dry and irritated). Avoid scrubbing too vigorously.

How to moisturize: Use a **lightweight, oil-free moisturizer** only on dry areas. Avoid anything containing heavy ingredients like mineral oil. If acne medication is making your skin dry, soothe it with moisturizer. Peeling and irritation is probably a sign that your treatment plan is too harsh.

How to troubleshoot:

- Treat blackheads and whiteheads with a **salicylic acid lotion or gel.** Apply a thin layer all over your face to de-clog pores—*and* prevent future comedones.

- **Pore strips** may also temporarily get the gunk out. It's best to use them only about once a week and only on thick-skinned areas (such as your T-zone). Never use a pore strip on broken-out areas—the irritation can make already inflamed spots worse.

- Zap zits by using a **benzoyl peroxide treatment** at night. Apply in a thin layer to areas where you tend to break out. The medicine can prevent zits you don't even know are in the works yet.

- Self-treating may not be for you. If your skin is dry or sensitive and broken-out (both skin types tend to react more acutely to many acne medicines), or if your acne gets worse after trying the do-it-yourself thing for six weeks, see a **dermatologist** (skin doctor).

Combination

How to recognize it: Your skin acts confused. The T-zone area may be shiny, while your cheeks are dry. Your face may seem oily and flaky at the same time.

How to cleanse it: Steer clear of cleansers designed for oily skin. Instead, go for a **mild nonsoap cleanser** and wash two to three times a day. If you apply a toner, swipe it only where your skin is shiny.

How to moisturize: Hydrate only where you need to (usually your cheeks) with an oil-free moisturizer, designed especially for confused skin. They contain ingredients to absorb oil, and also have light moisturizers that target dry areas.

How to troubleshoot:
- If your problem is oiliness combined with dry areas that look excessively red and/or scaly and flaky, it could be **seborrhea,** a condition caused by overactive oil glands. This can usually be controlled with an antiseborrhea treatment (available over the counter at the drugstore), but it's best to have the condition checked out by a dermatologist first.

Dry

How to recognize it: Your skin feels tight, sometimes irritated after washing. *Note:* Don't confuse the dryness and irritation acne medicines can cause with having dry skin. If you think your zit-zapper may be the culprit, stop using the products for a few days before trying to figure out your true skin type.

How to cleanse it: Don't wash your face more than twice a day—or three times, if you exercise. Use a **mild, creamy lotion cleanser** that leaves light moisturizers behind.

How to moisturize: After cleansing, slather on a **rich, creamy moisturizer** (a cream form tends to be more softening and soothing than a lotion), while skin is still slightly damp.

How to troubleshoot:

- Use a treatment containing the ingredient **alphahydroxy acid** to slough off dead skin cells.
- Once or twice a week, try an **exfoliating scrub** (one with synthetic granules that are smooth, round, and uniform is more skin-friendly than one made with rough natural grains derived from, say, apricot pits).
- At night, use a **humidifier**—it adds moisture to dry air, which may help hydrate your skin.
- If your skin is still desert-dry, see a dermatologist. He or she can determine whether you have a condition, such as **eczema** or **psoriasis**, that requires a prescription treatment.

Sensitive

How to recognize it: Skin frequently feels tight, dry, red, or irritated. In severe cases, rashes, blisters, or hives can crop up. Problems tend to occur when your skin is exposed to new products or to harsh temperatures.

How to cleanse it: Stick to **gentle, nonsoap washes** that are free of artificial fragrances and dyes. For a deep-clean feeling, skip the astringent and go for a gentler **alcohol-free toner** instead.

How to moisturize: Again, look for fragrance-free, dye-free lotions (anything white, as opposed to colorful, is a good bet). If your skin is still reacting to this kind of lotion, ask about preservative-free formulas at the health-food store. Some skins are sensitive to these chemicals, which are used to prolong a product's shelf life. The only downside to preservative-free products is that once opened, they only last about a month or so, compared with other moisturizers that last up to a year.

How to troubleshoot:

- If your skin freaks when you switch skin-care routines, be careful to test-drive only one new product at a time. Wait 7 to 10 days to make sure it doesn't cause a reaction before trying another new product.
- If a rash, blisters, or hives develop, see a dermatologist. He or she can do a patch test. Here's how it works: A patch soaked in the suspected offender is applied to clean, nonirritated skin to determine whether you're having an irritant or allergic reaction to a substance.

> *"Make your own scrub for dry skin by wrapping a handful of uncooked oatmeal in a washcloth. Dampen it with water and rub it all over your body when you're in the shower."*
>
> — DANA, Kentucky
> **seventeen** reader

The Right Way To Wash Your Face

Cleansing your face is the most crucial part of your skin-care routine. It may seem like a no-brainer, but lathering up the wrong way—or too often—can actually do more harm than good. Here's how to wash your way to beautiful skin:

- Pick the right cleanser for your skin type.

- Don't use the same scented or deodorant cleanser that you use on your body. Many of them contain detergents and fragrances that can aggravate facial skin.

- Treat your skin gently. Just as you wouldn't toss your cashmere cardigan in the washing machine with your jeans, you shouldn't scrub the delicate skin on your face too hard or use the same sponge or pouf you use on your body. Instead, use your fingertips or a soft, dampened cotton washcloth to gently massage in cleanser.

- Wash with lukewarm water—hot water is too drying.

- Don't fall for the myth that the more often you wash, the cleaner your skin will be. Twice a day is plenty for most skin types.

COMING CLEAN

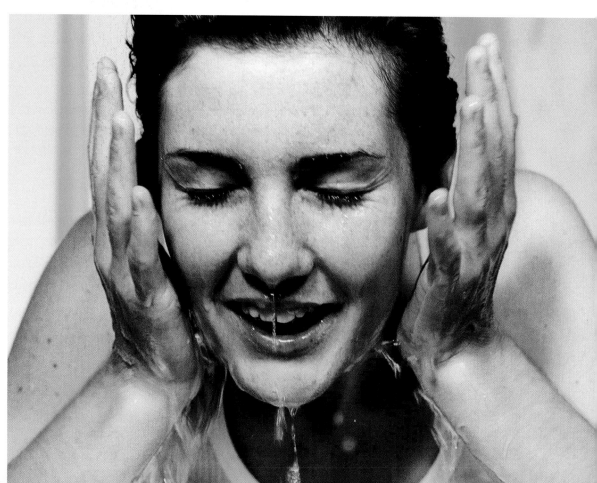

QUIZ:
SKIN MYTHS

HOW SKIN-SAVVY ARE YOU?
TEST YOUR ACNE ACUMEN!

1. You can get acne by:
a) Close contact with someone who has it.
b) Not scrubbing your face enough.
c) Worrying about a mid-term.

2. The fastest way to zap a zit is:
a) Keep the area clean and apply a medicine (like benzoyl peroxide) that will dry it up.
b) Squeeze the white stuff out of it.
c) Visualize it away.

3. What puts the black in blackheads?
a) A combo of dried oil, dead skin cells, and skin's own pigment.
b) Built-up dirt from improper cleansing.
c) Wearing lots of makeup.

4. Scarfing mass quantities of French fries:
a) Makes you break out more often.
b) Makes no difference when it comes to your skin.
c) Makes the people at McDonald's happy.

5. Dabbing toothpaste on a zit:
a) Dries it up.
b) Prevents cavities.
c) Can make it worse.

6. Getting a suntan:
a) Helps clear up pimples.
b) Aggravates acne.
c) Is a fast way to make problem skin look better.

ANSWERS:

1. (c) You can get acne from stress. The theory is that stress causes a shake-up in your hormone department. When your adrenal glands start producing more of the hormones adrenaline and androgens, your oil glands go into overdrive. Since you can't exactly stop stressing on command, practice smart, preventive skin care. Eat a balanced diet and choose skin-care products that are both **noncomedogenic** (meaning they won't clog pores) and **nonacnegenic** (meaning they won't cause acne). Acne is not contagious, nor does it require excessive scrubbing.

2. (a) Keeping a blemish clean and using acne medicine to dry out excess oil and kill bacteria are the best ways to zap a zit. **Never squeeze a pimple** (it can get infected and cause scarring).

3. (a) Contrary to popular belief, the black part of a blackhead is not dirt or residue from makeup, so you can't scrub it away. Blackheads crop up when your pores get clogged with dead skin cells and excess oils. Dermatologists think the dark stuff inside is the effect of your skin's melanin, or natural pigment, on this gunk.

4. (b) Unless you're rubbing junk food directly on your face, there's no evidence that scarfing greasy, creamy, or sugary foods leads to breakouts.

5. (c) Toothpaste, though drying, contains ingredients that can be superirritating to your skin. Forget those other home remedies, too. Eye drops can make the area around the zit unnaturally white and leave it even redder when the effect wears off. Hemorrhoid creams may shrink swelling, but the greasy formula can clog your pores. Best bet: Stick to medicines designed for zits.

6. (b) Catching rays may have a temporary drying effect on oily skin but the negatives far outweigh the positives: When skin is exposed to the sun, your natural sunburn protection kicks in and thickens your hide. That slows down the normal sloughing process and causes clogged pores. The result: Within two or three weeks, you'll begin to break out. Also, even the slightest sunburn can cause existing pimples to leave dark spots behind.

The Zit Files

Seventeen's beauty department receives enough questions about zits to merit an entire encyclopedia on the subject. It's not surprising when you consider the stats: According to the American Academy of Dermatology, **nearly twenty million teens nationwide currently experience some kind of acne.** That's because hormones tend to kick in during puberty and stimulate your oil glands to produce more of the slick stuff.

Here's a closer look at different kinds of skin sabotagers, and what you can do about them:

Blackheads and whiteheads

What they look like: Blackheads show up as clogged pores that are open at the skin's surface and look dark inside. **Whiteheads** appear as tiny, light-colored, firm bumps that are closed off at the skin's surface. Neither should be tender or sore to the touch.

Why they happen: Both blackheads and whiteheads are caused by a buildup of slow-shedding dead skin cells. When the gunk mixes with excess oil (a result of heredity and/or hormones), it clogs up pores.

What to do about them: The key to busting blackheads and whiteheads is to uncork clogged pores and speed up skin's natural sloughing process. Wash twice a day with a **salicylic acid cleanser.** At bedtime, apply a thin layer of a **salicylic acid formula** (available in 2-percent formulas over the counter) all over your face. Make sure to avoid the delicate skin under your eyes.

When to see a dermatologist: If your skin doesn't look clearer in three months, or if you see 50 to 75 comedones at one time. (Don't sweat the number—you'll know when the situation has gotten worse!) Your doctor may prescribe a stronger concentration of salicylic acid or a **retinoid lotion** or **gel**. Both work just below skin's surface to control and eliminate dead skin cells.

SAVING FACE

*"If it's going to be a hot and sweaty day,
go easy on the foundation or skip it all together.
Sweat mixed with makeup can clog your pores,
and clogged pores lead to breakouts."*

— JENNIFER, Virginia
seventeen reader

What they look like: Zits are usually raised and red, often filled with whitish stuff. They tend to feel irritated or sore to the touch. Dermatologists separate zits into categories based on their size and degree of inflammation. You may hear your doc refer to them as **papules** (the smallest kind), **pustules** (larger, inflamed, and filled with yucky white stuff), and **cysts** (the largest, reddest, sorest variety, often called underground zits because the material inside isn't close enough to the skin's surface to be squeezed out).

Why they happen: Zits start out as clogged pores. When oil and dead skin cells combine with fast-multiplying acne bacteria, your body's immune system kicks in and attacks. This causes an inflammatory response: redness, soreness, and swelling.

What to do about them:

- Wash your face twice a day with a gentle cleanser. Or, try one containing **antibacterial ingredients** (like **benzoyl peroxide** or **triclosan**), but stop using it if your skin gets too dried out.

- Apply a benzoyl peroxide product nightly. Start with a low concentration (look for ones that say 2.5 percent or 5 percent on the label). If these aren't effective, try a 10-percent benzoyl peroxide treatment—but be on the lookout for excessive redness, dryness, irritation, or peeling. You may find that your skin can only tolerate the medication when it's used every other day.

- Resist the urge to squeeze a zit. The pressure could rupture the pore wall beneath the skin's surface, creating a deeper, infected cyst that tends to leave a nasty dark spot—or even a real scar.

When to see a dermatologoist: If your acne doesn't improve within three months, or if you develop deep underground cysts (they usually crop up along the sides of your face, near your hairline). A doctor may prescribe a combination plan of attack that includes a topical and/or oral antibiotic (which helps control acne bacteria) or a stronger topical antibacterial medicine.

POP CULTURE

GOT A HUGE DATE... AND AN EVEN HUGER ZIT?

While squeezing and popping a blemish are among the biggest beauty no-nos around, we admit there are those occasions when you simply can't leave the house with an antlerlike protrusion coming from your forehead. But if you have to do some "home improvement," at least do it in the safest way possible. Try these legit emergency tactics we got from a dermatologist:

- Attempt to rid yourself of a zit *only* when there's white stuff inside that's so close to the surface that a warm compress can bring it out without applying any pressure. Place a warm, wet washcloth on the area every ten minutes for a couple of hours. This brings white blood cells to the area to speed healing. Never use your nails, a pin, or any other sharp implement to squeeze out the white stuff. If it's ready to come out, it will happen while you're applying the heat from the washcloth.

- If the pimple is still red after a few hours, apply ice to restrict blood vessels and reduce redness, but don't squeeze—it's not ready to come to the surface yet. Instead, apply concealer and cut your losses.

- If all else fails—and it's a superprimo occasion like the prom or your sister's wedding—ask your dermatologist if he or she can give you a painless cortisone injection to shrink your mondo zit.

Body acne

What it looks like: Any combination of blackheads, whiteheads, zits, or cysts. They usually show up on your chest, back, shoulders, upper arms, and/or butt.

Why it happens: For the same reasons as acne on your face, but also because of external factors, like sweltering temps or working out in tight, synthetic exercise gear (trapped sweat mixes with sebum and causes a pore-clogging film).

What to do about it:

- Clean the skin below your chin as carefully as you do your face.

- After a workout (or any excessively sweaty activity, like hanging out on the beach on a really hot day), shower as soon as possible with a **body wash containing salicylic acid. A long-handled back brush** helps with hard-to-reach areas.

- For blackheads or whiteheads, apply a **salicylic acid** product to the affected area. For zits, try **benzoyl peroxide.** The thicker skin on your back and shoulders can usually tolerate a high concentration, but a milder formula is better for sensitive chest skin.

- To prevent future breakouts, go for loose-fitting workout wear that's made of natural fibers such as cotton. If you have to wear a team jersey made of synthetic material, slip a cotton tee or tank under it. Keep in mind that some acne medications (especially benzoyl peroxide) can bleach clothing, so make sure your lotion is fully dry before getting dressed.

When to see a dermatologist:
If your skin doesn't respond to over-the-counter remedies, or the problem worsens, make an appointment with your doctor. He or she can prescribe retinoids, topical or oral antibiotics, or Accutane (a superstrong acne medicine sometimes used to curb below-the-neck breakouts).

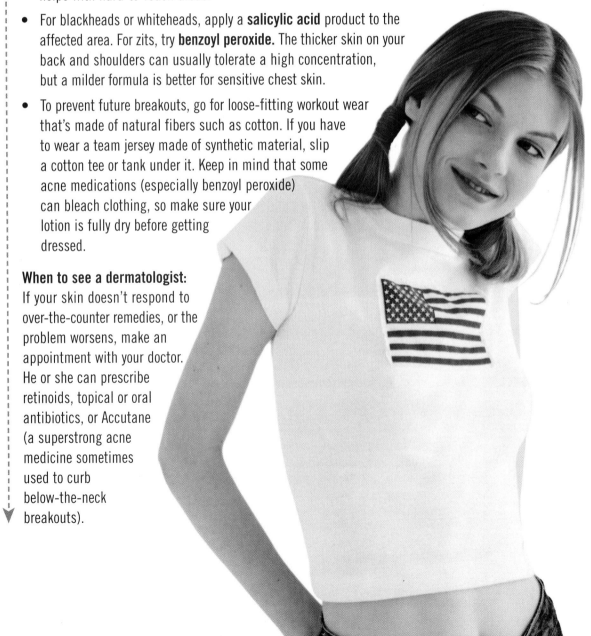

BEATING BREAKOUTS:
DOs AND DON'Ts

DO apply acne medication over your entire face (so it can battle potential blemishes while it treats what's already there).

DO keep bangs off your face when you exercise (the combination of sweat and the oils in your hair can clog pores).

DO hold the phone away from your chin (excessive rubbing can cause breakouts).

DO wear an oil-free sunscreen with a sun protection factor (SPF) of at least 15 or higher whenever you're outside.

DON'T eat lobster, shrimp, sushi (if it contains seaweed) or other iodine-rich foods *if* they make you break out. But don't stress too much about snacks like chocolate bars or fries (dermatologists say there's no proven link between these treats and acne).

DON'T pick at or squeeze pimples (it can make them bigger, and even lead to scarring).

DON'T wash your face more than two or three times a day (washing too much can overdry skin, possibly causing it to produce even *more* oil).

DON'T use heavy leave-in hair conditioners, gels, or mousses if you're prone to acne around your hairline.

DON'T rub or touch your face too much (it irritates skin, not to mention spreading dirt and bacteria).

DON'T experiment with "alternative zit-busters" like toothpaste, hemorrhoid creams, or eye drops (ingredients in their formulas can irritate broken-out skin, doing more harm than good).

I want to grow my bangs out, but I always seem to break out on my forehead. Without bangs, my zits will be way obvious. Help!

Your bangs may be causing your problem. If your scalp is oily, your bangs can absorb the oil, which can lead to breakouts. If your bangs rub against your forehead, the friction can irritate your skin and cause zits. Sometimes, heavy, sticky styling gunk can be a culprit in plugging up pores. What to do: Switch to a lightweight, rinse-out conditioner and, if possible, keep gels, mousses, and hairsprays away from your bangs.

If under-bangs acne pops up suddenly and is red and inflamed, you may be allergic to an ingredient in a styling product—even if you've been using the product for a few weeks. If you think you might be allergic, stop using any hair helpers you've bought in the past month.

Scar Wars

What most of us refer to as acne scars are actually dark or red spots left behind as souvenirs by inflamed zits. Doctors call them post-inflammatory pigmentation. They can last anywhere from several weeks to several months—even up to a year in some cases.

As a general rule, the darker your skin, the darker the spots will look and the longer they'll last. Persistent red spots can be more of a problem for fair-skinned people. Some degree of discoloration after a zit is inevitable, but picking and squeezing can make it linger longer.

The easiest temporary solution is to **cover spots with a good yellow-based concealer** until they fade on their own. To speed things up a bit, try products that contain exfoliating ingredients like **alphahydroxy acids, retinoids,** or **salicylic acid.** They slough away dead cells from the top layer of skin, bringing new, spot-free skin to the surface. Dermatologists can also help fade dark spots with prescription medicines, in-office micropeels, or laser treatments. No matter how you treat dark spots, it's a good idea to stay out of the sun as much as possible. UV rays can make dark spots even darker.

Real scars—actual depressions or pits in the skin—are rare and are usually caused by deep, cystic acne. Shallower scars can be minimized by a chemical peel, in which a dermatologist applies concentrated exfoliants that remove the scarred top layer of skin. Deeper scars have traditionally been treated by docs with dermabrasion (a high-intensity electric skin-buffing), but some dermatologists are now using lasers to "vaporize" scarred skin. Both cause some swelling and irritation while skin heals, but the new laser treatments tend to be more precise.

"If your skin is oily, cleanse it with a bit of fresh lemon juice once a week. Rinse immediately with lukewarm water."

— NICOLE, New Jersey
seventeen reader

DID U KNOW? Your T-zone may have more oil glands than the rest of your body, but you actually have oil glands from head to toe. The only exception: The palms of your hands and the soles and tops of your feet.

HOW TO FIND A DERMATOLOGIST

You've tried over-the-counter breakout-busters for six to eight weeks, and you're still seeing spots. You have deep, underground zits that won't go away. What do you do?

Make an appointment with a qualified dermatologist. He or she should be certified by the American Board of Dermatology.

To find a specialist in your area, ask your regular family doctor for a recommendation, or log onto the American Academy of Dermatology's Web site at www.AAD.org for more info. When you go for your first appointment, the doctor will examine your skin and take a medical history before prescribing an at-home treatment regimen.

Every month (the time of my period) I break out in the exact same spot. Is there anything I can do to head this off?

PMS-induced breakouts happen when hormonal shifts cause skin to produce more oil than usual. The hormonal blemishes that precede a period are usually of the bigger, deeper, underground variety. They tend to crop up in the same places: along the sides of your face, your jawline, and on your chin. While you can't do anything to control your hormones, you can practice preventive skin care. Applying a thin layer of a topical retinoid nightly all over the area where you tend to break out will help prevent pores from becoming clogged. Cystic acne (large, firm-feeling red zits) generally responds best to topical and/or oral antibiotics, which have to be prescribed by a dermatologist.

Don't Sweat It

You take a shower and slather on deodorant every morning—but by lunchtime, you've worked up a lather of your own (wet spots under your pits). Don't sweat it, you're not the only one. According to deodorant makers Procter & Gamble, nearly one in four women have what they describe as "severe perspiration dilemmas."

What's up with the wetness?

First, your sweating rate is just one more biological factor that's determined by genetics, so the amount you perspire has nothing to do with how many showers you did or didn't take that day. Sweating is how your body maintains its normal 98.6 degrees. There is no real cure for sweating, but these steps should help you keep dry:

- Use an **antibacterial soap** to stop bacterial growth before it starts. Sweat is mostly odorless water. However, warm crevices like your armpits provide the perfect environment for bacteria to grow—and that's what causes that funky smell.

- Pick the right odor-fighting product. An **antiperspirant** contains ingredients like aluminum salts, which actually block the underarm pores, preventing wetness. A **deodorant** simply masks your personal smell with its own scent. **Antiperspirant/deodorant** combinations do both jobs.

- All types of pit protectors are available in a variety of forms:
  - Sprays tend to go on lightest and dry fastest.
  - Gel solids and roll-ons are better for people with sensitive skin (the higher alcohol content in sprays can be irritating).
  - Sheer solids go on clear, so they don't leave any chalky white stuff on your clothes.

- When applying an antiperspirant or deodorant, apply the product evenly, covering your entire underarm area.

- If all else fails, see your doctor about a megastrong prescription-strength antiperspirant.

MAKING SCENTS

DID U KNOW? When you're really active or really nervous, you can sweat up to two liters per hour!

All About Fragrances

Sniff this out: Perfume does more than just smell good. No sense is more closely wired to memory or emotion than the sense of smell. That's why catching a whiff of your ex's cologne on the guy behind you in the cafeteria line brings back such powerful memories.

Your aroma of choice tells the world as much about your personality—or your mood—as the clothes you wear or the music you listen to. But with so many fragrances out there (not to mention the army of overzealous department store spritzers trying to convince you to sample them), it can be tough to decide which one is truly Eau de You.

Here are some scent-shopping dos and don'ts:

- **Don't** wear any fragrance when you hit the perfume counter. That scent will interfere with your ability to test-drive new ones.

- **Do** ask the sales associate if you can mist new scents on blotter cards (pieces of paper made especially for this purpose). Don't spray the scent directly onto your skin. It can be tough to remember which scent was which when you've got a different one sprayed on every appendage.

- **Don't** test more than six or seven scents in one shopping trip—your nose is likely to go on olfactory overload and lose its ability to discern between different aromas.

- **Do** collect as many free samples as you can. Spray them on (one per day) when you get home. See how you like the scent after a few hours—many start to smell different after they dry down (*translation:* when the alcohol evaporates).

Scent-Speak

Perfume: The most concentrated form of fragrance. It lasts the longest and tends to be the priciest. Dab it on your pulse points (the insides of your wrists), your neck and throat, behind your ears, even the backs of your knees.

Solid perfume: The same concentration of perfume, but in a "solid" cream or cream-to-powder formula that comes in a compact.

Perfume oil: Highly concentrated, these often come in roll-on bottles and are designed to be dabbed on very sparingly.

Eau de parfum: A slightly less concentrated version of perfume. It's stronger and longer-lasting than an eau de toilette and has a midrange price tag. Apply it the same way you would perfume—only you may need to reapply after a few hours.

Eau de toilette: A lighter, usually spray-on version of your favorite perfume. It tends to be more affordable. Spritz a light mist, or squirt some in the air and walk through it.

Cologne: Even lighter than eau de toilette. Often used for guys' or unisex scents.

Body mist: The lightest and least expensive form of fragrance. Body mists tend to be alcohol-free. They're designed to be misted all over your body and reapplied often. (Some formulas even have built-in moisturizing ingredients.)

Scent And The Season

Just as you swap your ski jacket for a bikini when the mercury rises, you may want to rethink your scent strategy. When it's hot outside, fragrances evaporate faster, causing them to smell stronger. So, in the summer, a subtle mist is probably plenty. You can also lighten up by switching to a less-concentrated form of your favorite fragrance (such as a body mist or lotion), or even sprinkling some scented talc in your sneakers.

During chillier weather, you'll probably need to dab on more fragrance and apply it more often to get the same effect. You might even want to experiment with a new scent altogether. For example, fragrance experts say spicier, heavier scents (like orientals, vanillas, and musks) can psych you into feeling warmer during frosty weather, while lighter, subtler scents (like florals, fruity florals, and green scents) are more refreshing during a heat wave.

BRIGHT IDEA

For an extra-cooling blast during warm weather, chill scents in the fridge before spritzing them on.

I love my friend's perfume, but when I tried it, it didn't smell the same on me. Why?

Several factors can affect the way a fragrance smells on different people. For one thing, perfume tends to linger longer and smell stronger on people with oilier skin. Dry skin absorbs the aroma more. Your diet can also play a role: If you eat lots of rich, fatty, or spicy foods, your skin may retain chemicals that intensify the way a scent smells. Likewise, some medications can alter your normal body chemistry. If you love your friend's aroma but find it's too strong for you, try switching to a lighter version of the same scent—or even a scented body lotion or shower gel.

EAU, NO!

WENT A LITTLE OVERBOARD ON THE PERFUME?
If your cat passes out when you enter the room, take the hint and try this quick fix:

Spritz the overaromatic body part with water or dab on some rubbing alcohol with a cotton ball. Both will make the scent evaporate faster.

Next time, be sure to hold spray-on scents at least six inches away from your skin. If possible, get a second opinion (your little bro will be brutally honest) before spraying on more. Your nose adjusts to the way you smell after a few minutes, making it tough to judge your perfume's potency.

DID U KNOW? The average teenager owns five or six different scents. Some prefer to switch depending on their moods, while others stick to a signature spritz for a few months, then move on to something new.

Hair Today, Gone Tomorrow

A surefire sign that warm weather is on its way: Letters start pouring in to **seventeen** about nixing unwanted body hair (is there any other kind?). Whether the fuzzfest shows up on your arms, legs, bikini line, upper lip, or elsewhere (don't worry, we've heard it *all*), you just want it gone—in as quick, efficient, and, you hope, pain-free a manner as possible.

If you've never shaved, waxed, or bleached before, you're probably wondering when—and how—to get started. As for when, it's a totally personal choice. **The only thing to keep in mind is that zapping body hair is kind of like eating potato chips: Once you start, it's hard to stop.** No matter which method of hair removal you choose, hairs tend to be more noticeable—stubbly and darker—as they grow back in. Be sure you're ready to deal with the maintenance factor.

Ready to get started? Here are the pros and cons of different fuzz-busting techniques:

Shaving

Best for: Legs, bikini area, underarms

How it works: The razor blade removes hairs at the skin's surface.

What you need:

- A razor (One with a slip-proof rubber grip and a built-in moisturizing strip works best.)
- Razor blades
- Shaving cream or gel (Both moisturize skin better than plain old soap.)

How to do it: Shaving works best during—or right after—a shower or bath, because wet hairs are softer and can be shaved off closer to the skin's surface.

Apply shaving cream or gel. Glide the razor over your skin using gentle, even strokes. Make sure your blade is sharp by changing it after every four or five shaves. If the blade is dull, you're more likely to press harder and shave over the same area twice, which can irritate skin and cause nicks.

DID U KNOW? Shaving doesn't make hair thicker when it grows in—it just looks that way. The deal: Shaving slices off hairs at skin's surface, which is actually at about the midpoint (or thickest part) of the hair shaft. Unless you pluck or wax, the rest of the hair remains under skin's surface. As it starts to grow back in, the first part you see is the thickest part. That's why stubble feels so prickly.

BARE ESSENTIALS

Different body parts call for different shaving strategies.

- When shaving your legs, move the razor in the opposite direction from the way hair grows.

- Your underarm hair grows in all different directions. To get a super-close shave, try shaving in the direction of a cross—up, down, and then from side to side. Relather each time you change direction so you don't irritate your skin. Wait at least thirty minutes before putting on deodorant. The odor-fighting ingredients can sting freshly shaved skin.

- When shaving your sensitive bikini area, shave in the direction hair grows to prevent irritation and ingrown hairs.

How long it lasts: Hair grows back in about two or three days, depending on how thick your hair is.

Pain factor: Nada, unless you cut yourself.

Bleaching

Best for: Lightening hair on the upper lip, arms, or belly. Only for medium to light skin tones (bleached-out hair can look too noticeable against darker complexions).

How it works: Chemicals in the bleach lighten hair instead of removing it.

What you need: An at-home bleaching kit (including: the active lightening ingredients, usually in powder form, plus a cream base to mix it with, and a spatula to apply the mixture).

How to do it: Most at-home kits give you a powdered form of the bleach to mix with a cream. When you've blended the right amount of each, spread the mixture onto the area you want to lighten. Leave it on for the prescribed amount of time before rinsing. Note: As with any chemical process, it's a good idea to do a patch test first on a small area, then wait 24 hours to make sure your skin doesn't get red or irritated.

How long it lasts: About two or three weeks.

Pain factor: None (but those with very sensitive skin may experience some irritation).

What's the best way to stand when you shave in the shower? I always seem to slip and cut myself.

If you shave in the shower, it's a good idea to stand on top of a slip-proof rubber tub mat—the same kind you sat on as a kid. If your shower is combined with the tub, rest the ball of your foot on the edge of the tub. If you lather up in a stall shower, invest in a plastic step stool and use it as a footrest. Whatever you do, don't place your foot on a tile wall (It's a fast track to Slipville!). Using a women's razor with a curved handle and a rubber grip may also help prevent slipups. If you're still feeling balance-challenged, try shaving while sitting in the tub, or sit on the floor with a cup of water handy to rinse your razor.

Depilatories

Best for: Legs, bikini area, face

How it works: Depilatories dissolve hairs just below skin's surface, allowing them to be rinsed away with water and a washcloth.

What you need:

- A depilatory cream, lotion, or foam. Be sure to choose a gentle formula if you'll be using it on a sensitive area like your face or bikini line.
- A washcloth
- A shower

How to do it: Allow hair to grow out for a few days before using. Apply a coat of the product to the unwanted hair. Follow the directions about how long to leave it on, then rinse under the shower, using a washcloth to wipe off hairs. Avoid using a depilatory right before you hit the beach or pool, or on any broken-out, cut, or otherwise irritated area.

How long it lasts: About a week to ten days.

Pain factor: Zero (but once again, it's best to try a patch test first to make sure your skin won't be irritated by the chemicals).

"When I shave my legs,
I use hair conditioner instead of shaving cream.
It keeps my skin really soft."

— AMANDA, Texas
seventeen reader

Waxing

Best for: Legs, abdomen, bikini area, eyebrows, face

How it works: Sticky wax is spread onto skin. When it hardens and dries, it gets quickly peeled off, pulling out hairs at the root.

What you need:

- A home waxing kit containing the wax itself (Some need to be heated on the stove or the microwave—follow the directions.)
- Fabric strips (Kits come with different sizes and shapes of strips designed for different body parts.)

How to do it: Heat the wax according to the directions. Spread it onto skin in the direction that hair grows. Apply fabric strips on top and wait for wax to harden and dry. Pull the strips off in the opposite direction from the way hair grows. Don't wax immediately after a bath or shower (it softens hair too much and makes it harder to grip and pull out).

How long it lasts: About four to six weeks. For best results, allow hair to grow to about a quarter of an inch before waxing again, because the wax needs something to grab onto.

Pain factor: Ouch! Waxing is kind of like pulling off a Band-Aid: The faster you do it, the less stinging you'll feel. But keep in mind that the larger the area you're waxing, the more prolonged your torture will be. If you have a low pain threshold, you're probably better off either visiting a professional waxer at a salon, or choosing another method altogether.

Electrolysis

Best for: Small areas like eyebrows, upper lip, chin

How it works: An electrologist inserts a tiny needle into the hair follicle to destroy the root with a mild electrical current.

What you need:

- An appointment with a certified, licensed professional (Electrolysis can't be done at home.)
- Plenty of time (Each hair is removed individually, so larger areas can take several appointments.)
- Plenty of cash (Electrolysis can cost as much as $75 per hour.)

How to do it: Just sit back, dream of the offending hairs being permanently zapped, and let the pro do her job.

How long it lasts: Forever—electrolysis is the only permanent method of hair removal.

Pain factor: Pretty major, though you'll only have to endure it once.

Grin And Bare It!

Now that you've nixed the fuzz factor, it's time to address some other stuff that may make you swimsuit-phobic. Body bummers like bikini-line bumps, stretch marks, and cellulite can happen to anybody, even supermodels (we've seen it—really!). So check out the facts on these totally common concerns, then stop stressing and hit the beach!

Bikini-line bumps

These nasty red spots around your bikini line happen because the skin there is ultrasensitive and the hair there tends to be coarse and curly. This combination causes ingrown hairs—when the hair grows around and back into your skin.

To clear things up:

- Prep your skin by exfoliating with a lotion containing alphahydroxy acid and by scrubbing gently with a washcloth or nylon pouf before using any hair-removal method. This will help to free your hair follicles of any blockage, so your hair has a better chance of growing out straight instead of curving in.

- If you wax, do it on dry skin—it's much less irritating.

- If you use a depilatory lotion, soak the area in the tub for a few minutes to help loosen the follicles. Pat skin dry before applying the cream or lotion.

- After hair removal: Swipe your bikini line with a toner containing salicylic acid or a postshave lotion designed to prevent ingrown hairs.

- If you do get bumps, don't pick them. They can get infected. Instead, use an over-the-counter hydrocortisone cream to reduce the redness and swelling. Nix shaving and waxing for a week or two, until the red bumps clear up. If your red spots are still visible and you're planning a day at the beach or pool, throw on a pretty sarong or a pair of board shorts and forget about them.

Stretch marks

Stretch marks are purplish or whitish lines that usually show up on your breasts, hips, or tummy. They are formed when the elastic fibers of your skin's inner layers are stretched faster and farther than usual by a quick change in your body's shape (like when you develop hips and breasts or when you have a rapid weight gain or loss). Whether you get stretch marks or not depends on heredity.

What to do about them:

- The good news: The lines may appear purplish at first, but they'll gradually fade to pink, and then turn to skin color, like a scar.

- A lot of moisturizing lotions and oils claim to improve the appearance of stretch marks. But they probably work best if applied before a growth spurt, which is next to impossible to predict.

- If stretch marks are very noticeable, ask your dermatologist about treatments that help heal scars.

Cellulite

Cellulite is pockets of uneven fatty tissue that give your skin a puckered appearance—usually on the hips and thighs. While eating a super-fatty diet and skimping on the exercise can worsen its appearance, cellulite tends to be genetic. That's why some rail-thin track stars have it, and some couch potatoes don't.

What to do about it:

- There are a lot of cellulite "treatments" on the shelves, but they only temporarily improve its appearance by tightening the surface skin.

- Your best bet—no matter what your DNA—is to eat a healthy low-fat diet, drink plenty of fluids, and exercise regularly.

"If you're nice on the inside, you'll become beautiful to other people on the outside, too."

— KRISTEN, Washington
seventeen reader

Everyone says I should drink 8 glasses of water a day. Is it really true? If I do, I'll be spending more time in the bathroom than the classroom!

Many actresses and models swear by guzzling as much water as they can get their hands on, and they're on the right track: H_2O keeps skin well hydrated and helps keep your body's metabolism moving along (though it's not a miracle cure for acne). If eight glasses sounds like way too much for your bladder to bear, increase your intake a little more slowly. Try to replace caffeinated colas, teas, and coffees with water (squirt some lemon juice in to give it more flavor), and carry around a bottle to swig from throughout the day.

The Tan Commandments

Okay, let's get this part over with: The words "safe" and "tan" just don't go together. Unprotected sun exposure can lead to gross stuff like premature wrinkles and (much worse) scary skin cancers. No matter how healthy you think you look with a beach-girl glow, the only safe way to get one is from a bottle, tube, or compact. Here are ten smart ways to safeguard your skin from the sun's harsh rays…and still have a blast outside:

SUN SMARTS

Always use a sunscreen with at least a sun protection factor (SPF) of 15—even if you already have a base tan or you have naturally dark skin. Even dark skin needs protection—besides the risk of skin damage, sun exposure can make dark spots darker and cause uneven skin tone.

Don't forget to hit often-neglected spots like your lips, ears, the back of your neck, the tops of your feet, even the part in your hair. Scary factoid: Skin cancer that pops up on the lips and ears is the fastest-spreading and most dangerous type.

Put on way more sunscreen than you think you need. An ounce (or a really big handful) is what skin docs recommend.

Don't rub sunscreen into your skin till you can't see it or feel it anymore. You'll rub off too much, and it won't protect you as well. (Fret not: The white stuff will sink in within minutes as the lotion dries.)

Remember to wear sunscreen under your T-shirt. A dry white tee has an SPF of 6 or 7, but when it gets wet, it's reduced to an SPF of 1.

Trash last summer's sunscreen and get some new stuff. Why? An unopened tube stays good for up to three years, but the minute you use it, the SPF factor starts to oxidize (translation: It won't work as well).

Don't wait till you hit the beach to apply your sunscreen. Smooth it on at home before you put on your suit and you'll be sure to cover the often-missed skin around the edges of your straps.

Use sunscreen whenever you're outside, even if you're only walking from the mall to your car. Sun damage is cumulative, meaning even brief minutes of exposure add up.

Check your moles frequently. If you notice irregular shapes or borders, color changes, or anything larger than a pencil eraser, ask your doctor to check them out right away. Any of these could be an early warning sign for skin cancer.

Don't go outside unprotected because you think your sunscreen is making you break out. Find a formula that's oil-free and says "noncomedogenic" and/or "nonacnegenic" on the label. If your acne-prone skin can't tolerate any sunscreen, save face by seeking shade.

QUIZ: SOLAR SENSE

BEFORE YOU BREAK OUT THE BABY OIL AND THE REFLECTORS, TEST YOUR TANNING IQ.

1. Cloudy days are best for outdoor activities, since you don't have to worry about sunburn.

a) True
b) False

2. The SPF (sun protection factor) of a sunscreen tells you:

a) How much longer it takes your skin to burn while wearing it than if you weren't wearing any sunscreen at all.
b) How many times a day you should apply it.
c) The number of hours you'll be protected.

3. If you put on sunscreen with SPF 8 over one with SPF 4, you'll end up with a protection factor of:

a) 12
b) 8
c) 4

4. The damage done to your skin when you're fifteen can cause wrinkles to show up when you're:

a) Twenty-five
b) Thirty-five
c) Forty-five

5. The only "safe" way to get a tan is:

a) In a tanning bed at a salon.
b) With a sunless tanning lotion.
c) Building up a "base" tan a little bit at a time.

6. Sunless tanning lotion works by:

a) Speeding up your skin's own natural tanning process.
b) Coating your skin like makeup.
c) Temporarily dyeing the top layer of your skin bronze.

ANSWERS:

1. (b) It's important to wear sunscreen even on cloudy days, since up to 80 percent of the sun's rays can shine through haze.

2. (a) If it takes your skin only ten minutes to start burning without sunscreen, an SPF of 15 will allow you to stay in the sun 150 minutes (or 15 times longer) than if you weren't wearing any sunscreen.

3. (b) Forget what you learned in math class—SPF numbers don't add up to produce a higher number. The highest SPF you put on is the one that counts.

4. (a) Sun damage can show up as soon as ten years after exposure, in the form of leathery skin and wrinkles.

5. (b) Tanning beds work with UVA light, which, while it doesn't necessarily burn your skin like UVB rays, can cause wrinkles and skin cancer. And when it comes to building up a base tan, keep in mind that any skin darkening is a sign of sun damage.

6. (c) Don't be fooled by the faux bronze: Self-tanning lotion just dyes the top layer of skin, so it doesn't provide any natural protection from the sun. You still need a high-protection sunscreen.

Sunscreen Shopping Made Easy

Need a clue when it comes to buying the right sunscreen? Consider these factors when you're cruising the SPF aisle:

➤ **The basics:** You've already read about the numbers game (at least SPF 15 for medium to dark skin, SPF 30 for pale skin). Another thing to look for on the label are the words **"broad spectrum"** or **"full spectrum."** This means that the sunscreen protects you from both the sun's aging UVA rays and burning UVB rays. Both of them can contribute to skin cancer. (Shopping tip: Look for ingredients like Parsol 1789, also called Avobenzone, and/or zinc oxide.)

➤ **Your skin type:** Like cleansers and moisturizers, sunscreens come in formulas for different skin types:

- Oil-free, noncomedogenic lotions or gels for oily or acne-prone skin
- Moisturizing lotions for dry skin
- Chemical-free formulas (they use physical ray-blockers, like titanium dioxide or zinc oxide, instead of chemicals) for sensitive skin

To protect your lips, go for a balm or stick that packs at least an SPF of 15.

➤ **Your sun style:** Pick your product depending on how you spend your time outdoors:

- If you're into water sports, choose a waterproof formula.
- If you're always on the court, pick a sweatproof sports formula that won't run into your eyes when you go up for a spike or smash a serve.
- If you're off to camp or going hiking, pack a combo sunscreen/insect repellent.

DID U KNOW? The darker your skin is, the more built-in protection it has from sun damage. Skin's darkness is determined by its amount of melanin, a pigment that provides a natural sun protection factor. But no matter how dark your skin is, don't skimp on the kind of SPF that comes out of a bottle—every complexion is susceptible to the premature aging and increased skin cancer risk that comes with catching rays.

FEELING THE BURN?

If you wind up with a sunburn in spite of your best efforts, skip the oils and heavy moisturizers (they can trap heat under skin and make the burning feeling worse). Instead, go for after-sun soothers containing aloe vera and Vitamin E. Take a cool shower or a soothing oatmeal bath. Be sure to wait until the burn dies down before shaving (burned skin is so sensitive and puffed up, you won't get a close shave anyway).

RASH RESPONSE

If you break out in a rash or blisters after sun exposure, don't assume sunburn is the culprit. Redness, itching, and irritation could also be a sign of photosensitivity (an allergic reaction triggered by mixing certain medicines or ingredients with sun exposure). Symptoms may even occur up to forty-eight hours after sunning. What might not mix well with UV rays:

- Certain prescription drugs (ask your pharmacist)
- Certain acne medicines, either topical or oral
- Some fragrances
- Some soaps and dandruff shampoos
- Foods such as parsley, celery, lime, and figs (when they come into contact with skin)

How To Fake A Tan

Okay, so a real tanfest is totally out.
But that doesn't mean you can't get a great glow without frying your skin!
Check out these safe, sun-kissed options:

Self-tanning lotion

How it works: Self-tanners deliver color that mimics the effects of the sun (without the damaging rays) by temporarily darkening the outermost layer of your skin.

How long it lasts: The color is waterproof and fades gradually after a few days.

Which one is right for you: Tanners produce a range of hues, from light gold to Caribbean copper, depending on how much skin-darkening ingredient (called DHA) they contain. The key to a believable faux tan is picking the right shade for your skin tone:

- If you're dark or olive and you want dramatic results, try a dark formula.
- If you're fair, layer on several coats of a light or medium product (a more pigmented formula could produce results that are too orange for you).
- If the product isn't labeled with a shade, assume it will produce a medium hue (when in doubt, do a test run on a small, hidden area of skin).

Other cool options:

- **Tinted self-tanners**—they go on bronze, so you can see any streaks and blend them in before the dye goes to work.
- **Built-in SPF**—so you're protected when self-tanning on the beach or by the pool.
- **Quick-drying formulas**—they let you get dressed faster.

Goof-proof tan plan:

1. Begin by getting rid of dead skin cells the day before you apply self-tanner. Use a gentle scrub. Pay particular attention to knees, elbows, knuckles, and ankles (the dye in self-tanners tends to cling more to dry, rough skin and turn those areas darker).

2. Apply a few thin, even coats instead of one thick, gloppy coat. Blend the lotion evenly over your skin with upward strokes.

3. Wash your palms afterward with soap and water.

4. Be sure the lotion is dry before you get dressed (DHA can stain clothing or sheets).

5. Self-tan once or twice a week to maintain your desired hue.

TANNING TIP When applying a self-tanner to your face, don't just stop at your jawbone—go all the way down to your neck so there won't be any obvious line. Also, blend lotion right up to—but not into—your hairline, since the darkening ingredient can also darken light hair. Go easy on areas where you're naturally paler (like the insides of your arms).

Bronzer:

How it works: Bronzers are copper-colored makeup. They give skin a temporary tanned look, but they're not waterproof.

How long it lasts: Until you wash it off, sweat a lot, or go swimming.

Which one is right for you: Like blush, bronzers come in several forms:

- **Powders** are great for oily skin and delivering a matte finish.
- **Creams** and **creamy sticks** give a more dewy glow.
- **Gels** are sheer and natural looking.

Shade is also important: Some bronzers are one-shade-fits-all, while others come in a range of hues. For the most natural look, **choose one that's just a few shades darker than your natural skin tone.** For a sparkly look, go for one with a bit of shimmer in it.

Goof-proof tan plan:

1. Apply bronzer wherever the sun would naturally hit your face—across your cheekbones, nose, forehead, and chin.

2. If you're using powder, streakproof it by lightly applying regular face powder before dusting on bronzer with a fat makeup brush. Tip: Blow on the brush or tap it against your hand first to remove excess color before stroking it on.

3. If you're using a cream, stick, or gel, dot it onto bare skin—or smooth a bit of moisturizer on first.

4. Keep in mind that sun-kissed color that stops abruptly at the jawline looks about as natural as rainbow eye shadow.

5. Blend well with a dry makeup sponge or velour puff. Gels set really quickly, so don't wait to rub them in or they may be too stubborn to blend.

it makes up 15 percent of your body's total weight!

SPA TREATMENTS

Ever wonder what glamour girls do at the superluxe (and often, superexpensive!) pamper palaces called spas? A day is often spent with soothing stuff like facials, body scrubs, and mud masks.

Sounds good—doesn't it? Does it really work? It's hard to say if spa days actually make your skin look better in the long term, but the treatments certainly feel great! And feeling great always helps you to look fabulous.

Want in on the spa action? Whether you're trying to chill out after midterms or do some pre-prom beautification, check out these do-it-yourself beauty treats—hey, you can even invite your friends over and make a party of it!

Facial

What it does: Deep-cleans pores. Professional facials usually involve steaming, cleansing, using a scrub or exfoliator of some sort, and applying a mask based on your skin type.

What you need:

- A mild cleanser
- An exfoliator designed for the face. It should have small, synthetic grains—they're less irritating to skin than rougher natural grains.
- The right mask for your skin type
- A toner or moisturizer

How to do it yourself:

1. Skip the home-steaming. Doing it for too long or with water that's too hot can weaken the walls of your pores, causing them to rupture. It also makes you sweat. Both of these are bad news for acne-prone skin. Instead, suds up with a gentle cleanser.

2. Apply the exfoliator to damp, just-washed skin, concentrating on areas where dead skin accumulates (like your T-zone). Avoid using scrubs on the delicate skin under your eyes and around your lips.

3. Apply a thin layer of the mask. Kick back and relax while the mask does its thing (it usually takes ten to twenty minutes, but check the package for details).

4. Rinse with lukewarm water.

5. If you have oily skin, follow with a toner, which will remove any traces of the mask and also leave your skin fresh and tingly.

6. If your skin is dry, follow with a moisturizer.

RISKY BUSINESS Occasional facials are fine if your skin is clear. They're not a great idea if you're acne-prone or already broken out. The friction from grainy scrubs can up the irritation factor. The wrong kind of mask can clog pores (if you're under a dermatologist's care, always check with your doc before putting *anything* new on your face). Also, giving yourself a facial the day of a special occasion, like the prom, can be risky: Breakouts sometimes follow when pore-clogging gunk is drawn to skin's surface. It's best to try the treatment at least one week before the big event.

DID U KNOW? Not only are girls more sensitive than guys, they're literally more thin-skinned. Female skin is actually thinner than male skin, causing it to be more reactive to external factors like hot or cold temperatures or chemical irritants.

Body Polish

What it does: Banishes super-rough spots on feet, legs, knees, and elbows; makes skin feel satiny-smooth all over.

What you need:

- A moisturizing bath gel
- An exfoliating scrub or salt rub
- A washcloth, nylon pouf sponge, or exfoliating gloves (lose the loofahs and natural sea sponges—they're major bacteria magnets!)
- Body lotion

How to do it yourself:

1. Pour bath gel into a tub of warm water and soak for a few minutes.

2. Lather up with the scrub.

3. Use a wet washcloth, pouf sponge, or gloves to apply the grains in a circular motion. Focus on rough, thick-skinned areas like your knees, elbows, and feet. Be especially careful when it comes to the more delicate skin on your chest. (If your skin is easily irritated or broken out below the neck, skip the scrub and choose a body wash containing alphahydroxy acid.)

4. Rinse off under a warm shower.

5. Pat skin with a towel (rubbing removes too much moisture) until it's almost dry.

6. Slather on a rich moisturizer.

MASK APPEAL

HERE ARE SOME HINTS TO HELP YOU CHOOSE THE RIGHT FACE MASK FOR YOU:

- Clay or mud masks can help dry up oily skin and leave behind a temporary tightening effect on pores.
- Creamier moisturizing masks are best for hydrating dry skin, but can be too heavy for oily or acne-prone complexions.
- Calming masks contain anti-inflammatory ingredients to soothe sensitive, irritated skin and reduce redness.

Mud Treatment

What it does: Sloughs off dead skin, tightens pores.

What you need:

- Enough mud mask to coat your body. Look for mud or clay masks that contain mineral-rich ingredients like **kelp** (a natural astringent that purifies skin) or **kaolin** (the cleansing ingredient found in clay). Steer clear of muds with mineral oil or real mud if you're broken out anywhere on your body.

How to do it yourself:

1 Apply a thick layer of mud from your neck down to your to your toes.

2 Leave it on for about ten or fifteen minutes (follow directions on the package).

3 Rinse it off with a washcloth in the shower.

*"After washing your face, splash it with icy cold water. Your skin will **really** glow!"*

— DINA, New Jersey
seventeen reader

*A*fter I used my new strawberry shower gel, my skin got red and itchy. Does this mean I'm allergic to it?

Not necessarily. It may just be an irritation, which is a common response to superscented products (especially during cold-weather months, when skin is drier and therefore more sensitive). Stop using the new product ASAP, and apply an over-the-counter hydracortisone ointment to the area to soothe itching and reduce inflammation.

If redness and itching don't disappear in a week, contact a dermatologist, who can determine whether you've got an allergy.

Either way, its best to give your skin a break and stick to a fragrance-free product. But beware: "Unscented" isn't the same thing as fragrance-free. Unscented products contain a masking scent that covers up the smell of the ingredients and can be irritating to sensitive skin.

TEN THINGS IN YOUR FRIDGE THAT CAN BE GREAT FOR YOUR SKIN

1 AVOCADO: When mashed into a paste, moisturizes dry skin.

2 CUCUMBER: Put slices over stressed-out, irritated eyes.

3 OATMEAL: When cooked and mixed into a mask or added to the bath, calms irritated or sun-burned skin.

4 APPLE: When it's mashed into a mask, the acid in it deep-cleans oily skin.

5 HONEY: When added to a mask, hydrates parched skin.

6 MILK: Add a cup of the powdered variety for an ultra-moisturizing bath.

7 YOGURT: Makes a great mask for balancing combination skin.

8 LEMON JUICE: Acts like an astringent for oily skin when added to a mask (but can be irritating to dry or otherwise sensitive skin).

9 SESAME OIL: Pour some into warm water to soften and moisturize dry hands or feet.

10 EGGS: The whites make a great face mask.

Skin Cheat Sheet

Ready for a quick recap?
Here are the crucial points to remember when it comes to
scoring glowing, gorgeous skin:

- Choose the right products for your skin type, and stick to your regimen.

- Limit lathering up to twice a day. Overcleansing can dry out skin and cause it to produce more oil.

- When using zit medicine, apply a thin layer all over the acne-prone area. This will help to prevent future breakouts while healing what's there now.

- Avoid overdoing it with acne-fighting treatments. Using too many medicated cleansers, astringents, spot treatments, and masks at once can irritate problem skin.

- Never squeeze a zit! It can cause scarring.

- Protect your skin from premature aging and skin cancer by applying a sunscreen with an SPF of at least 15 before going outside.

NAILS
chapter 4

Nail It

Your nails get noticed. Whether they're long and red or short and pink or ragged and dirty, nails make an impression—they tell people about who you are and how you care about yourself. Even if you'd rather polish your corner kick or your personal Web page than your nails, dignified digits call for a little shaping and grooming. Here's everything you need to whip your nails into shape:

- Acetone polish remover
- Cotton pads and cotton swabs
- Emery boards (fine-grade for shaping, rougher grade for shortening)
- Nail clippers
- Round buffing disc
- Cuticle-conditioning oil
- Cuticle-remover lotion
- Orangewood stick or washcloth
- Clear base coat
- Nail polish in your favorite color
- Clear top coat
- Quick-drying top coat or speed-drying spray

Whether you like to wear your tips diva-long or short, bare, and keyboard-friendly, **seventeen** has tons of tips for magnificent manicures—and perfect pedicures, too.

EIGHT STEPS TO A GREAT MANICURE

THE NAIL FILE

1 Wash your hands with soap and water. Wipe off any old polish with a cotton pad soaked in an **acetone polish remover.**

2 Use a **fine-grade emery board** to gently shape nails. Keep the file on the white part of your nail. File from each side toward the center, but moving the emery board in one direction only. (*Note:* If you want to shorten long nails ASAP, use a **clipper.** Be sure to file any sharp edges.)

3 Smooth the edges of your nails and the surface ridges with a **round buffing disc.** Don't overdo the buffing—remember, buffing removes layers of the nail.

4 Massage a **conditioning cuticle oil** all around the edges of your nails, paying special attention to hangnails. Then soak hands in warm, soapy water. Towel dry.

5 Apply **cuticle remover lotion** to the sides and base of nails. Cover the tip of an orangewood stick with cotton. Use the stick or a **damp washcloth** and gently push back cuticles. Then remove excess lotion from your nails with a cotton pad soaked in polish remover.

6 Brush on a **clear base coat.** Allow to dry for one minute.

7 Apply **two coats of polish.** Clean up outside-the-lines polish with a cotton swab dipped in remover.

8 To give your handiwork staying power, apply a **clear top coat.** Some top coats are quick-drying. If yours isn't, seal your shade with a **speed-drying spray.**

DID U KNOW? If you change your nail polish more than once a week, you will risk drying out your nail bed. Your nail bed is the part at the base of your nail that is responsible for nail growth.

H ow do I make my nails dry really fast? I hate sitting and waiting!

Start by applying your polish in two very thin coats instead of one thick, gloppy one. To ensure a thin application, turn the bottle upside down and roll it gently between your palms before opening it. After dipping the brush in the polish, wipe the excess lacquer on the rim of the bottle before stroking it on your nail. When you're finished, try a speed-drying top coat. Another option: Check out one of the new fast-drying polishes that combine the colors you want with formulas that set within a minute or two.

"Giving yourself a manicure once a week can help your nails grow. And remember, always carry a nail file, and never bite or pull at snagged nails."

— JENNY, New York
seventeen reader

Shaping Up

Before you reach for the emery board, decide which nail shape will look best on your nails. In general, the shape of your nails should mirror the shape of the base of your cleaned-up cuticles. The shape can be **oval, square,** or a **sharp U-shape.** Also, nail length depends on the shape of your hands and fingers. Here are a few pointers:

- **Broader nails** tend to look better with a classic **oval** shape.

- **Narrower nails** look hipper when they are **squared off with round edges.**

- **Superlong nails** can make long, thin hands look too clawlike.

- **Really short nails** will make small hands with short fingers look stubby.

WARNING Filing or buffing your nails when they're wet is a major no-no. Waterlogged nails are weaker, and can split and tear more easily.

Salon Smarts

You didn't spend all that time folding sweaters at the mall or baby-sitting the neighbor's whiny kids so you could blow your earnings on a less than hygienic manicure. But that's just what you could wind up with if your nail salon makes one of the cleanliness mistakes below. Here's how to see if your salon is up to snuff:

- Make sure that your manicurist disinfects all the tools. Tools should be soaked in a disinfectant solution for at least 10 minutes. Spraying tools with a disinfectant doesn't kill all the germs.

- If you plan to get professional manicures on a regular basis, invest in your own set of tools. Either bring the tools with you each time or ask the salon to store them for you until your next appointment.

- Never allow a nail technician to cut your cuticles. Cuticles protect the nail bed and cutting them increases the risk of infection and hangnails. Instead, ask her to use a cuticle cream, which softens the skin, so the cuticles can be gently pushed back.

"Use a nail buffer to smooth out ridges on nails. It'll look like you have clear polish on all the time."

— ROBYN, Canada
seventeen reader

DID U KNOW? The nail on your middle finger grows faster than all the others, and your thumbnail grows at the slowest rate. What's more, the nails on the hand you use most grow faster than those on the opposite hand.

Is there really a difference between expensive department store nail polish and the less expensive drugstore kinds?

Drugstore polish can hold up just as well—sometimes, even better—as the expensive department store or salon kind, providing you apply it right. (For example, did you use a base coat to help it adhere, and a top coat to help seal it?) The only big difference between drugstore and department store polish is the choice of color and the packaging. All nail polishes are pretty much created with the same ingredients. So when to splurge on a pricier polish? When you've simply got to have that glittery lavender or you've fallen in love with a polish's fancy packaging and are willing to pay more for that cute little adornment around the bottle.

The Three-Stroke Technique

For flawless nail polish application, here's an easy technique that really works: Dip the nail polish brush in the polish and wipe it off on the rim of the bottle (this helps the polish go on more evenly). Brush a quick, light stroke up the center of your nail. Without redipping, brush a stroke up the left side of your nail. Brush a stroke up the right side of your nail. Do redip the brush before you polish the next nail.

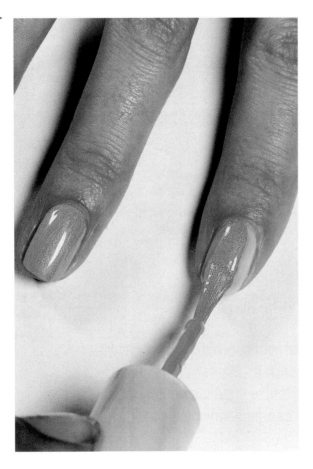

POLISH POINTERS

For best results

Begin by painting inward from your pinky nails on both hands, leaving your thumbs and index fingers for last (it's harder to maneuver the brush when the fingers you're gripping it with are wet). If you're right-handed and you're trying to polish the nails on your right hand with your less-coordinated left hand, rest the heel of your left hand firmly on the edge of a table while stroking on color.

"Apply a coat of clear polish or nail strengthener at least once a day, but don't remove the old coat. The thicker the polish, the better—it keeps your nails hard. At the end of the week, take off all the polish and start again."

— JULIA, New Jersey
seventeen reader

DID U KNOW? Polish is actually good for your nails. Enamel acts as a barrier against the elements. It seals in the natural moisture in your nails to prevent them from becoming dry and brittle. *Warning:* Nail products that contain the solvent toluene or the hardener formaldehyde can be very drying. Also, for some people, formaldehyde can cause an allergic reaction.

The Perfect Paint Job

Whether you go for bright red, glittery, or nearly nude lacquer, different polishes can pose different kinds of problems. For a perfect paint job every time, check out these do-it-yourself manicure secrets:

Make **sheer polish** streakproof by waiting until the first coat is totally dry before applying the second coat. *Another streak buster:* Apply an opaque base coat in a neutral beige-pink that's close to your own natural nail color.

Keep **dark polish** from staining your nails by applying a base coat underneath it.

Remove stubborn **glittery polish** by soaking a strong cotton pad (a wimpy tissue won't do the job) in an acetone-based remover. Firmly press the pad against your nail. Hold it there for a few seconds before trying to swipe off the polish. Remember that the larger the pieces of glitter, the harder they'll be to remove. Next time, apply a base coat underneath the sparkly stuff so the glitter sticks to the first coat of lacquer—not to your nails.

Nix **air bubbles** by starting with oil-free nails (wash with an oil-free cleanser and clean carefully around your cuticles with a nail brush or old toothbrush. Never shake the polish bottle. Instead, turn it upside down and roll it between your palms to thin the polish before you apply it.

MANICURE 911

STILL-WET SMUDGES
Quick Fix: Drop a small amount of polish right on the smudge. Immediately smooth the edges a bit with your fingertip (a cotton swab will leave fuzzies behind). Allow to dry completely.
Next Time: Try a quick-drying formula or use a fast-drying spray.

ALREADY-DRY CHIPS
Quick Fix: Don't have time to start from scratch? Then try putting a little polish remover on your fingertip and run your fingertip around the chip. This helps to soften the polish around the chip. Put a drop of polish directly on the chip. Allow the drop to dry, then polish over the entire nail.
Next Time: Apply a clear top coat every night over colored lacquer to prevent chipping.

Base coats and top coats look the same. Do I really need to buy both?

Base coats and top coats are both clear, but they serve different functions. Base coats are thicker and stickier so they can help your polish cling better. Top coats are thinner and contain certain solvents that help them dry more quickly. Top coats are designed to be harder so they protect the polish underneath from chipping. Some combo base coats/top coats are formulated to get both jobs done, but if a product is labeled top coat or base coat, it's best to use it only for that purpose.

Finger Painting

Got designs on a nail style that's more unique than basic polish? You don't have to be a Picasso or Matisse to get creative with your tips. Here are some cool techniques to try:

Decals

What They Are: Preprinted designs that adhere to your nails (either bare or on top of a coat of polish).

Different Types:

- Temporary tattoolike decals are cut out from a sheet of designs. You soak the decal in water before placing it on your nail. (A pair of tweezers makes picking up and applying smaller designs easier.)
- Stickerlike decals peel off and attach right to your nails.

The Know-How: If you are applying decals to unpolished nails, make sure your nails are clean and dry. Wipe your nails with polish remover first to make sure there are no traces of cuticle oil or lotion. If you are applying decals over polish, make sure the polish is completely dry first. Apply a coat of clear polish over your decals to extend their life.

Freestyle nail art

What It Is: Painting unique designs on your nails.

What You Need: A few colors of polish, a very fine-tipped brush (you can pick one up in an art supply store or use a very small makeup brush), and polish remover to clean the brush between colors.

The Know-How: You can paint on bare nails or on polished nails that are completely dry. Try polka dots, hearts, stars, zebra stripes—whatever! When you're finished, seal your works of art with a clear top coat.

Stencils

What They Are: Cut-out designs to place on your nail and fill in.

What You Need: Like decals, stencils come in kits with different designs.

The Know-How: Pick a shape you like, stick it to your nail, then polish in the cut-out area only. When the polish is completely dry, peel off the stencil to reveal the design. Make sure polished nails are dry before trying to stick on the stencil.

Nail jewels

What They Are: Sparkly rhinestones or other gems to dazzle your nails.

What You Need: The stones. You can buy nail-decorating kits that come with a variety of stones plus their own adhesive.

The Know-How: Stick rhinestones directly onto a coat of freshly applied polish before it dries, or use the adhesive supplied in your kit to stick stones to already dried polish or bare nails. *Warning:* Only use special nail adhesives to stick jewels on your nails!

French Manicure

A French manicure is only as French as French fries or French toast, but the concept is très cool: The white part of your nail gets brightened with a coat of opaque white, while your entire nail gets polished with a sheer neutral polish (beige or pink). It gives nails a clean, natural look. For a funkier French twist, trade pink and white for more out-there colors. Try putting the darker color on the tips and the lighter color below. Here's how to get the chic French thing going:

1. Start by covering your nails with a base coat.

2. Polish your nails with one coat of the polish of your choice.

3. If you are an ace at art class, you can try to trace your nail tips freehand with the second color. Make sure to wipe the brush on the rim of the bottle to remove gloppy excess polish—you are painting a very thin line.

4. If you goof, fix messed-up polish with a cotton swab dipped in remover.

5. Unable to draw a straight line? Artistically challenged? No problem: You can buy French manicure kits that come with both polish colors you'll need, plus stick-on stencils that help you place the white right where you want it.

NAIL CARE ON THE RUN

STOCK THESE FINGER-FRIENDLY ITEMS IN YOUR LOCKER OR BACKPACK:
- Emery board (for filing away nicks that could turn into tears)
- Nail glue (for fixing big tears)
- Strengthening top coat (for applying a lunchtime coat to weak nails)

Hue Are You?

A RAINBOW OF COLORS

White during winter? Dark burgundy for summer? When it comes to nail color, toss the rules out the window—pretty much anything goes. That said, there are a few factoids you may want to consider when choosing new hues:

- **Dark** or **bright polish** tends to make nails look shorter.

- **Pale polish** gives the illusion of length.

- **Shimmery metallic polish** draws attention to ridges and imperfections on the surface of your nails.

- **Sheer neutral shades** are really hard to mess up, and it's less noticeable when they chip.

DID U KNOW? No matter how futuristic your silver polish, painting your nails is hardly a new concept. Since the days of Cleopatra, glam girls have been grooming their nails and decorating them with color. Word has it Cleo chose dark colors made from plant-based dyes.

Color Theory

According to the Pantone Color Institute (the pros who study colors), viewing different hues can have an effect on our moods. This won't work with your lipstick shade—you would have to constantly look in the mirror or be a serious contortionist to see the color often enough for it to affect you. But it's certainly worth a try with your nail polish. Check out the supposed attitude-altering powers of these pigments:

- **Blue** or turquoise are said to be supersoothing and calming when you're stressed.

- Yellow or orange are thought to be mood-elevating and happiness-inducing.

- **Red** has a rep for revving up your heart rate and igniting passionate feelings.

- Green is supposed to improve your focus and concentration skills.

- Pink is perfect for first dates and Valentine's Day—it puts you in a romantic groove.

Mixing It Up

Want to satisfy your weekly (okay, daily) craving for a new polish shade…but find yourself inconveniently lacking in the funds area? Put the polishes you already own to work in a whole new way—blend different colors and textures of polish together to arrive at a totally unique hue.

Use an empty polish bottle (swish a bit of remover inside, pour it out, and let the inside dry completely first) to mix two or several colors together. Chances are that some of your combos will turn out looking like mud, but keep trying. The right mixture of certain colors can create a dynamic, totally unique color. If you want to experiment with a look before whipping up a whole batch, simply layer coats of different polishes on your nails. For fun, try glitter on top of metallics, or sheer shades on top of opaques.

During the summer, I like to wear sheer pink polish, but it always seems to turn yellow after a couple of days. What's the deal?

Some polishes undergo chemical reactions when they are exposed to the sun's rays, and this makes them change color. If your pale polish is going too golden, try protecting it with a top coat containing an ultra-violet inhibitor (a fancy name for a built-in sunscreen).

Scoring A Perfect 10: A Trouble-Shooting Guide

THE BREAKING POINT

Problem	Solution
Ridges	To even out a ridged nail's surface and get a smoother application of polish, gently buff with a round buffing disc. Then apply a ridge-filling base coat. Ridges are occasionally caused by certain medications or health problems, so if they persist, check with your doctor.
Weakness, Splitting	Keep weak or brittle nails as short as possible. Nourish them daily with a cuticle treatment and seal in moisture with a protective, hardening polish. File away any nicks with a superfine-grade emery board to prevent snags without weakening nails further. Mend deeper tears with a drop of nail glue (be sure to remove polish first) or a nail wrap.
Dry, Peeling Cuticles	Moisturize the area regularly with a conditioning cream or oil. Don't cut cuticles. Push them back gently with a cotton-covered orangewood stick after soaking your nails for a few minutes in soapy water. If you must trim a hangnail (a tiny—but usually painful—tear in the cuticle or surrounding skin), soften it first with a cuticle remover lotion. Then carefully snip with nail scissors or cuticle nippers and apply an antibiotic ointment.
Stains, Spots	To remove surface stains (the yellow coloring that red or burgundy polishes can leave behind), lightly buff nails with a round buffing disc. If spots persist, try a stain-removing cleanser (available in the nail aisle at the drugstore), or use a cotton swab dipped in hydrogen peroxide. Avoid future stains by wearing a base coat under dark polishes. FYI: The nicotine in cigarettes can cause yellow stains on nails—one more reason to kick the habit!

Keep Your Gloves On!

Cold-weather nail care

It's freezing outside and the cold, dry weather is making your hands feel like sandpaper. On top of that, your cuticles are peeling and your nails are breaking. It's gotten so bad that you're considering wearing your gloves all the time—even when you're inside! To get a handle on the problem, follow these finger tips:

- It's important to keep cuticles well-moisturized, since that's where nail growth begins. Prevent painful hangnails by applying daily **cuticle conditioner.** Massage an **emollient cream** or **oil** into the base of each nail at night.

- When polishing, coat brittle nails with a **moisturizing base coat.**

- Resist the urge to switch shades constantly. The less frequently you use polish remover, the better it is for your nails.

- To soften your hands, slather on a **rich hand cream** as often as possible. Always protect your hands with a pair of **gloves** or **mittens** whenever the outside temperature drops below 40 degrees.

- At bedtime, try this **overnight hand treatment:** Slip just-moisturized hands into a pair of cotton gloves (or socks, in a pinch) and wear them while you sleep. The trapped heat from your body helps the moisturizer penetrate deeper.

BRIGHT IDEA

To keep cuticles from getting too dry and cracking, soak your nails in warm olive oil once a week for ten minutes and massage the oil into your cuticles.

"If your nails are weak, try keeping them short for a period of time. It gives them a chance to get stronger and healthier."

— KRISTEN, Washington
seventeen reader

Go With The Faux

It's prom night and you just have to have long nails, but you're a chronic biter. You spiked the volleyball during gym class and your perfect ten became a perfect nine. Or you usually keep your nails on the short side, but you want to test-drive glam-length ones without waiting for them to grow.

There are several ways to give your natural nails an artificial boost—in either length or strength. The following tip-fixers are on the menu at professional nail salons and, in many cases, are available in do-it-yourself home kits. Keep in mind that while salon services may be more expensive than picking up a kit at a drugstore, home improvement is complicated and you'll need to follow the instructions very carefully to avoid infection.

Tips

What They Are: Pieces of already-hardened plastic shaped like the ends of your nails.

What They Do: Give nails instant length.

How They Work: You or the manicurist choose the right size tips for your fingers. Then the tips are attached with a special glue. When the glue dries, tips are shaped with an emery board and polish is applied on top.

Do-It-Yourself Advice: Before you begin, spread the tips out in finger order to avoid having to dig into the package while your nails are drying. Start with your pinky and finish with your thumb (this frees up your thumb and index finger for most of the application process). If you mess up, soak nails in acetone polish remover, then wipe with a cotton swab to remove any glue. Begin again on clean, dry nails.

Acrylic nails

What They Are: A liquid coating that hardens when it's painted on top of your own nails.

What They Do: Strengthen weak or brittle nails; lengthen nails.

How They Work: Acrylics are created by painting over your entire natural nail with a mixture of liquid and powder resins. When the solution hardens, nails are buffed smooth and shaped with a file. If acrylics are being used to lengthen nails, a special plastic form is placed under the edge of your own nail, then acrylic mixture is extended onto the form. When it hardens, you can shape your new, longer nails.

Do-It-Yourself Advice: To get acrylics—and tips—to attach better, buff the nail surface lightly with a disc file. Remove acrylics and tips after about two weeks to check that your natural nails are healthy underneath. Allow nails to breathe for at least a week between applications.

NAIL HELPERS

DID U KNOW? To be filed under "Life Isn't Fair": Guys' nails grow faster than girls'.

Wraps

What They Are: A tiny piece of silk or linen.

What They Do: Strengthen weak nails; mend actual tears in nails.

How They Work: A piece of fabric is glued onto your nail with a special nail glue. When the glue dries, the patch gets buffed with a disc, then polish is applied on top. Some salons offer liquid wraps, in which a polish containing nylon fibers is dabbed on the tear, allowed to dry, then buffed to smooth the surface.

Do-It-Yourself Advice: Wraps can be tricky to smooth out; it's best to leave this service to the pros.

Press-on nails

What They Are: Fake nails that stick on top of your own nails.

What They Do: Give you instant long-looking nails.

How They Work: Fake nails usually attach with double-sided sticky tape. Since they can't be reshaped with a file, you have to rely on matching existing shapes in the kit to your nails. Look for a kit that comes with a variety of shapes and sizes.

Do-It-Yourself Advice: Make sure there is no air space between the press-on nails and your own nails. Dirt can get trapped in air pockets and cause infection.

I bite my nails and my hands look horrible. I've tried to stop, but I always starting chewing again. Please help!

Nix the urge to nibble by painting on a bitter-tasting polish (nail-care companies make products specifically for this purpose). Still biting? Put your money where your nails are. Forking over the cash for weekly manicures is a great incentive to stop munching on your professionally pampered tips (salon manicures cost about $8 to $15). Most nail salons also offer an artificial acrylic coating—a flexible, tooth-proof material that protects nails while they grow in. *Another tip*: Zero in on your prime chomping time (watching TV? talking on the phone?) and, if possible, wear a pair of gloves while doing these things.

The Perfect Pedicure

Think slapping on a quick coat of polish before slipping on your sandals qualifies as a pedicure? Think again. A true pedicure lives up to its name: a cure for gnarly tootsies. That means not only prettifying your toenails, but giving the rest of your feet—soles, heels, calluses, and all—equal time, too. Here's how to put your best foot forward:

1. Soak your feet in warm, soapy water for ten to fifteen minutes. While you're soaking, clean under and around your toes with a nail brush.

2. Use a smoothing pumice stone or foot scrub to soften hardened, rough skin on your heels and soles. While you scrub, rub away tension by massaging each of your toes individually. Rinse feet and dry thoroughly.

3. Trim each toenail straight across with toenail clippers, leaving nails long enough to reach the tips of your toes. Don't clip the sides of your nails—cutting corners can lead to ingrown toenails and infection. If toenails need shaping, file them with an emery board.

4. Clean up cuticles by applying cuticle remover lotion and gently easing skin back with a damp washcloth or cotton-covered orangewood stick.

5. Massage a moisturizing foot lotion into toes and soles. Clean excess lotion from toes with a cotton pad soaked in polish remover.

6. Use a foam rubber toe separator to keep toes spread apart. Apply a base coat, two coats of polish, and a top coat. Allow at least one minute of drying time between each coat.

7. Wait at least 45 minutes before putting on shoes or socks.

TREAT YOUR FEET

SOOTHING SOAKING SOLUTIONS

ADD ANY OF THE FOLLOWING TO WARM WATER FOR A FANTASTIC FOOT BATH:

- Chamomile tea
- Warm sesame oil
- A few drops of peppermint oil
- Epsom salts
- Baby oil or any bath oil

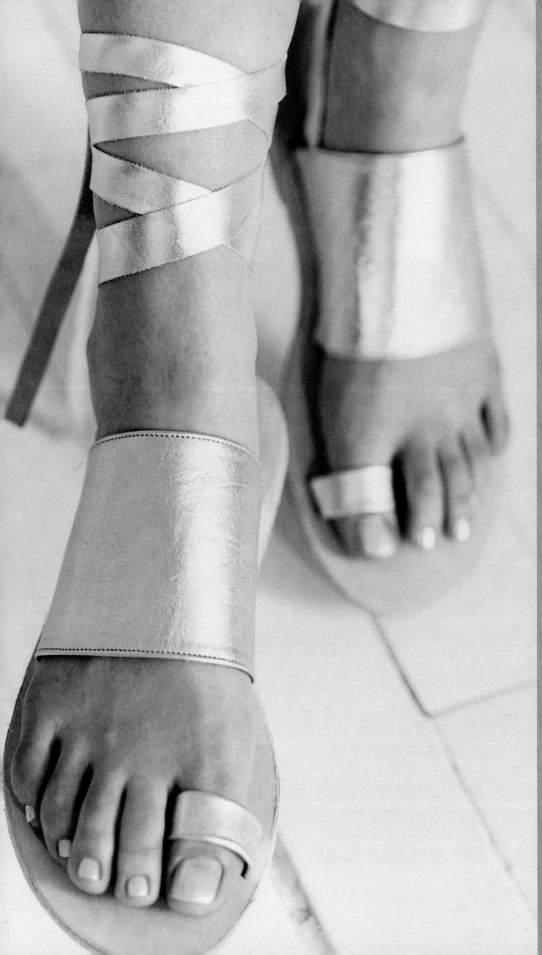

Dear Seventeen:

I'm on my school soccer team, and my feet are covered with calluses. Now it's summertime, and I want to wear strappy sandals. Is there any hope?

When skin is repeatedly exposed to friction (like the rubbing of that certain spot on your pinky toe against the inside of your cleat), it thickens and hardens, creating a callus. Get goal-kicking tootsies sandal-worthy by soaking feet in warm water for ten minutes to soften skin, then scrub rough areas with exfoliating grains. Gently smooth stubborn calluses with a foot file (like an emery board but coarser and larger) or a pumice stone (a block-shaped exfoliating file). If calluses are too tough to smooth by yourself, visit a podiatrist (foot doctor) to have them removed safely. To prevent future calluses, check to make sure that your shoes—especially athletic shoes—fit properly.

Foot 411

Got stinky feet? Don't worry—you're not alone. We've all had to leave our sneakers out on the porch to air after a long day's wear. That heinous stench is the result of the sweat on your feet mixing with the bacteria that crops up when you've been wearing your shoes and socks for a while. Here are some steps you can take to fight foot odor:

- Start by giving your feet a good wash—when you wake up and before you go to bed. Don't forget to scrub between your toes.

- Dry your feet thoroughly. Massage in a minty lotion for odor protection.

- Apply a deodorizing powder or spray made especially for your feet. You can also sprinkle on a little cornstarch or baking soda.

- Keep feet fresh and dry by slipping special insoles in your shoes to absorb perspiration.

- Always wear cotton socks with sneakers.

- Stick to shoes made of leather, nylon, or canvas (they let feet breathe easier).

- To prevent athlete's foot, remove socks immediately after exercizing or excessive sweating. Wash and dry between toes.

TOE TROUBLE

An ingrown toenail results when the edge of the nail starts growing inward and digs into the surrounding skin, causing inflammation, redness, pain, and even infection.

What can cause it:

- clipping nails too short

- angling the corners on the nail or jamming feet into too-narrow, too-tight shoes

- If you get a painful ingrown nail, see your doctor or a dermatologist—he or she can determine whether it needs treatment to heal. In the meantime, wear comfortable shoes with plenty of toe space. And in the future, trim nails straight across instead of on an angle (if trimming leaves behind sharp corners, file them gently).

Nails Cheat Sheet

Ready for a quick recap?
Here are the crucial points to remember when it comes to getting perfect nails:

- File nails only in one direction to avoid splitting and hangnails.

- Moisturize cuticles daily with a cream or oil. Gently push them back. Cutting cuticles can lead to infection.

- Apply several thin coats of polish instead of one thick, gloppy coat. Allow each coat to dry completely before painting on the next.

- The shape of your nails should mirror the shape of your cuticles (once they're cleaned up, that is).

- Be careful when applying fake nails of any kind yourself. Follow directions and be sure nails are clean and dry before you begin.

- Trim toenails straight across to prevent ingrown nails.

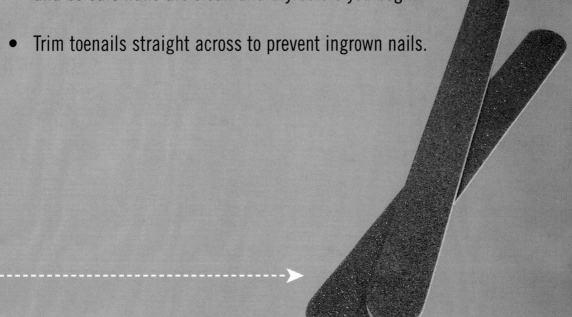

Afterword

Congrats—you're now a total beauty guru. We hope this book has answered every makeup, skin, hair, or nail question you could possibly think of. If you want more beauty info or the scoop on the latest *How to Be Gorgeous* tips and trends, be sure to check out www.seventeen.com.

Now that you've finished *How to Be Gorgeous*, you're ready for me to impart the last—and most important—byte of beauty wisdom I have to offer. No, it's not a secret spell for scoring straight hair or long-lasting lipstick. But it is easy, fast, and totally free. Are you ready?

Smile.

It may be the ultimate cliché, but it happens to be true. No matter how expertly you blend your blush and apply your eyeliner, a negative attitude sends out vibes that are anything but beautiful. (Just ask any one of the mood-challenged models we have turned down for photo shoots!)

Not only will cracking a smile make you *look* better, but studies show the mere act of grinning can actually make you *feel* better. Any guy who has ever had to work up the nerve to ask a girl out will tell you that happiness is way more attractive than, say, smoky eyeliner or perfectly plucked eyebrows. Go ahead and give your outside your best shot. But always remember that **real beauty**—the glowing, can't-take-my-eyes-off-of-you kind—**has to come from within.**

Index

Acknowledgments

First, I'd like to thank **seventeen**'s editor-in-chief, Patrice Adcroft, for giving me the opportunity (and the hiatus from my regular responsibilities) to write the book I've wanted to work on since coming to **seventeen** seven years ago. Major thanks also to my editor, Heather Alexander, for helping me to organize a massive amount of beauty info into a fun, user-friendly guide, and to Andrea Chambers at **seventeen** for her insight, ideas, and encouragement. I would also like to thank Alison Jurado, Kellee Monahan, Aimee Herring, and Jana Siegal, also at **seventeen**, for their contributions.

This book would not have been possible without the research and hard work of **seventeen**'s talented beauty staff, past and present, with whom I've been fortunate enough to work. Thanks especially to Jennifer Laing, Laura Kenney, Jennifer McIlhenny and Sophie Knight, and to all of our amazing interns.

A big thank you to my family and friends for their support, enthusiasm and, most importantly, babysitting help, especially Barbara and Philip Brous, Marion White, Alvis Anderson and Anne Martelli.

Last, but certainly not least, thanks and much love to the Guevara boys—Charlie, Alexander, and Andrew—for always making me feel beautiful on the inside (even when I'm a mess on the outside!).

Photography Credits

seventeen books...
for the times of your life

Wherever books are sold.

Books created and produced by Parachute Publishing, L.L.C., distributed by HarperCollins Children's Books, a division of HarperCollins Publishers.
© 2000 PRIMEDIA Magazines Inc., publisher of **seventeen**. **Seventeen** is a registered trademark of PRIMEDIA Magazines Finance Inc.

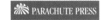 PARACHUTE PRESS   seventeen    HarperCollins*Publishers*

Don't miss this chance to Win a Trip to New York and hang out with the editors of your favorite magazine!

GRAND PRIZE
- ▼ 3-day, 2-night trip to New York City
- ▼ Meeting with the editors of seventeen
- ▼ Fabulous makeover at New York City salon

3 FIRST PRIZES
- ▼ Personal astrological reading

50 SECOND PRIZES
- ▼ Cool makeup bag filled with makeup

- - - - - - - - - - - - - Enter to Win - - - - - - - - - - - - - ✂

Name: _____

Date of Birth: _____

Parent/Legal Guardian (if minor): _____

Address: _____

Phone: _____

Fill out and mail to:

Arrowhead Promotion & Fulfillment
P.O. Box 8188
Grand Rapids, MN 55745-8188

One entry per person. No purchase necessary. You must be between the ages of 13 and 21 to enter. See back for official rules.

Seventeen Sweepstakes Official Rules

NO PURCHASE NECESSARY. SWEEPSTAKES OPEN ONLY TO LEGAL U.S. RESIDENTS BETWEEN THE AGES OF 13 AND 21 YEARS AS OF 9/1/00. Employees (and their immediate families and those living in their same households) and all officers, directors, representatives, and agents of HarperCollins Publishers, Parachute Properties, seventeen magazine, and any of their affiliates, parents, subsidiaries, advertising and promotion and fulfillment agencies are not eligible. Sweepstakes starts 9/1/00, and ends on 1/1/01. By participating, entrants agree to these official rules.

To Enter: Entries will be used by HarperCollins only for purposes of this Sweepstakes. Hand print your name, complete street address, city, state, zip, and phone number on this official entry form or on a 3 x 5 card and send to: PO Box 8188. Grand Rapids, MN 55745-8188. Limit one entry per person/family/household. One entrant per entry. HarperCollins Publishers is not responsible for lost, miscommunicated, late, damaged, incomplete, stolen, misdirected, illegible, or postage-due mail entries. Entry materials/data that have been tampered with, altered, or that do not comply with these rules are void. Entries become the property of HarperCollins Publishers Inc., and will not be returned or acknowledged. Entries must be postmarked by 1/1/01, and received no later than 1/8/01.

Drawing: Winners will be selected in a random drawing held on or about 1/9/01 by HarperCollins Publishers, whose decisions are final, from all eligible entries received. Winners will be notified by mail on or about 1/15/01. The prizes will be awarded in the name of minor's parent or legal guardian. Odds of winning depend on total number of eligible entries received.

Prizes: Grand Prize: One (1) Grand Prize Winner will receive a trip to New York City for two (2) people (winner and parent or legal guardian) for 3 days, 2 nights at a date to be determined in Spring 2001. Prize consists of round-trip coach class air transportation to and from winner's nearest served airport (U.S. citizens residing in the U.S. at the time of the trip), standard hotel accommodations for one room, two nights, a day with the editors of **seventeen** magazine, and a makeover at a New York City salon to be chosen by sponsor. Total approximate retail value (ARV) is $3,000.00. Travel/accommodation restrictions may apply. All other expenses not specifically stated are the sole responsibility of the winner. Winner must travel with winner's parent/legal guardian if winner is a minor in his/her state of residence. Travel and use of accommodation are at risk of winner and parent/legal guardian and HarperCollins, Parachute, and **seventeen** magazine do not assume any liability. First-place prize: 3 First Place Prize winners will each receive a personal astrological reading by an astrologer chosen by sponsor, the time and place to be determined at sponsor's sole discretion. Approximate retail value (ARV) is $500.00 each. Second-Place Prize: 50 Second Prize Winners will each receive a special makeup bag filled with makeup. Approximate retail value (ARV) is $10.00 each. Total value of all prizes is $5000.00. In the event Grand Prize Winner is unable to travel/accept prize during time specified, Grand Prize Winner shall be considered to have irrevocably forfeited prize and an alternate grand prize winner will be selected. If any prize is not available or cannot be fulfilled, HarperCollins, Parachute, and **seventeen** magazine reserve the right to substitute a prize of equal or greater value. Prizes are not redeemable for cash value by winners.

General Conditions: By taking part in this Sweepstakes entrants agree to be bound by these official rules and by all decisions of HarperCollins Publishers, Parachute Publishing, and **seventeen** magazine. Winners or their parents/legal guardians, if minor in his/her state of residence, are required to sign and return an Affidavit of Eligibility and Liability Release and where legal, a Publicity Release within ten (10) days of notification. Failure to return documents as specified, or if prize notification or prize is returned as nondeliverable, may result in prize forfeiture and selection of an alternate winner. Grand Prize Winner and his/her travel companion must sign and return a Liability/Publicity Release prior to issuance of travel documents. Sweepstakes is subject to all applicable federal, state, and local laws and regulations and is void in Puerto Rico and wherever else prohibited by law. By participating, winners (and winners' parents/legal guardians, if applicable) agree that HarperCollins Publishers, Parachute, **seventeen** magazine, and their affiliate companies, parents, subsidiaries, advertising and promotion agencies, and all of their respective officers, directors, employees, representatives, and agents will have no liability whatsoever, and will be held harmless by all winners (and winners' parents/legal guardians, if applicable) for any liability for any injuries, losses, or damages of any kind to person, including death, and property resulting in whole or in part, directly or indirectly, from the acceptance, possession, misuse, or use of the prize, or participation in this Sweepstakes. Except where legally prohibited, by accepting prize, winners (and winners' parents/legal guardians, as applicable) grant permission for HarperCollins Publishers, Parachute, **seventeen** magazine, and those acting under their authority to use his/her name, photograph, voice and/or likeness, for advertising and/or publicity purposes without additional compensation. Taxes on prizes are solely the responsibility of the winners. Prizes are not transferable and cannot be assigned.

Prize Winners' Names: For the names of the Winners (available after 1/15/01), send a self-addressed stamped envelope for receipt by 1/31/01 to Arrowhead Promotion & Fulfillment, PO Box 8105, Grand Rapids, MN 55745-8105.

Sponsored by HarperCollins Publishers, New York, NY 10019-4703.